TWO CENTURIES, TWO COUNTRIES,

TWO HUSBANDS

A Memoir by Luisa Stigol, M.D.

Publisher's Information

EBookBakery Books
Contact; michael@ebookbakery.com

ISBN 978-1-938517-38-9

Author contact: luisastigol@comcast.net

About the Cover Photo: The photograph of Dr. Stigol at work at
Children's Hospital in the Department of Pathology appeared in 1972 as
part of the cover of *The Boston Sunday Advertiser*, a periodical. The photo
was part of an illustrated article: "*Latins in Boston: two sides to a growing
population.*"

Acknowledgments

To Odile and my doctors who kept me alive. To those who showed interest in the idea of this book. To all the teachers who enriched my life, my father especially.

Table of Contents

Dedication

To my children, grandchildren and little great-granddaughter

1

Childhood and Boston

I was never the typical grandmother who told family stories to her grandchildren. My grandchildren grew up far away from me even though I made sustained efforts to cover the distances that kept us apart. But my profession and financial resources limited our contact. I did not see one of them for seven years. Now they are adults and we feel close to each other, our communication supported by this marvelous era of Skype and cell phones. I wanted to share our family story with them, so I include it below.

I was born into a loving, middle-class family in Buenos Aires in 1930. My father, Abraham, a Russian Jew, emigrated to Buenos Aires with his family when he was three. He was born in Shpola, a shtetl near the old city of Kiev in the heart of what was then Russia and is currently independent Ukraine. Jews settled in small communities where Yiddish was the spoken language. The political turmoil of that time resulted in frequent pogroms. Jews were stoned and their property destroyed. As a result, my father's father, my grandfather Max, a school teacher; and his three brothers, left for America, the land of promise. My grandmother Rachel, pregnant at the time, stayed behind with eight of their ten children. Sophia, the eldest, had already gone to the United States by herself.

The four brothers "Shtiegall" were ready to embark for the U.S. from a European port, Hamburg I believe, when it was discovered that my grandfather had developed conjunctivitis, a transient inflammation of the mucosal lining of the eyes. That changed his destiny. The American immigration authorities, afraid of blindness-causing diseases like trachoma, did not allow him to board the ship with his brothers. Desperate to find a safe haven for his family back in Kiev, he had no choice but to sail alone on the boat which had accepted him — bound for Argentina. His arrival in Buenos Aires in 1910 was auspicious: the city was celebrating the centenary of its independence from Spain. Conditions were far better than those he had left behind in Russia. Unfortunately, my grandfather's profession, as a Yiddish teacher, was of little use in his new land. Instead, he became a peddler, aided by earlier Jewish arrivals who provided him with merchandise on credit which he sold door-to-door. He earned little money, mostly being paid coins for his merchandise. In a deformation of the Spanish word for counting those coins, "contar," these peddlers were called "cooantenics." The word remains part of the Jewish folklore of that time.

Despite his modest income, my grandfather managed to bring his large family to Argentina. My father's three older brothers, Carlos, Israel and José, helped Max support the family.

My father's family eventually moved from Buenos Aires to Bahía Blanca, a port town on the Atlantic. Catalina, one of my father's five sisters, along with David and my father, attended the local high school. My father cherished the memory of those years when good teachers introduced him to Dante's *Divine Comedy*, Italian and French, including poems by Lamartine that he could recite from memory to the end of his long life. Catalina complained about getting poor grades after studying a lot - while my father studied little and received excellent grades. That turned out to be a source of much pleasant teasing between the two. A highlight of my father's high school years was the first-place prize he won as a freshman – he was eleven – playing Charles Chaplin at a "Mi Careme" competition organized by the city. I have a photograph that appeared in a local newspaper, of a thin, mustachioed youngster wearing baggy pants, over-sized shoes, and a round, black hat tilted to one side. He appears in the photo with the vague expression of the dispossessed vagabond and looking very Chaplinesque.

In Bahía Blanca, my grandfather graduated from peddler to furniture store-owner but did not distinguish himself as a tradesman. The only one in the family with business sense was José. (I will refer to him as Joseph; he never accumulated riches due to his chronic generosity. Whenever he bought shoes or dresses for his own daughter, Annie, he bought some for me as well. When I graduated from medical school, he presented me with the money I needed to build an office in my apartment.)

After completing high school, Abraham and David, who remained close throughout their lives, moved to Cordoba to study medicine. Their loyal and hardworking older brothers financed their education. My paternal grandparents followed later. I recall that their apartment was impeccably clean. My grandmother Rachel decorated her home and took care of her guests in a refined manner that suggested some affluence in her European girlhood. (I say relative affluence because Jews who lived in shtetls were never truly affluent.) My Aunt Sophia and my father inherited their good taste from her. Grandmother Rachel, short and stooped perhaps from keeping house and feeding ten children, was also a consummate mother. It was said that she prepared different meals for each of her children to suit their various tastes.

Max, my paternal grandfather, was already bald when I knew him. His manner was gentle and relaxed. After his experience with the anti-Semitic violence that forced him to leave his native Russia, he decided that religion divided people and stopped practicing Judaism – although he never relinquished its moral teachings. My father was strongly influenced by my grandfather's philosophy of tolerance for the beliefs of others.

Unlike my father, my beautiful mother, Eugenia, was born in Argentina. As a child, I knew her brother Isaac, her maternal grandparents and their seven children and grandchildren. Like my father's family, my mother's ancestors had also come from Russia – in their case, Odessa. One main fact emerges from the stories my mother told me about her childhood. For reasons she never discussed–poverty perhaps–my grandmother Luisa, for whom I am named, died tragically while still very young. At the time of her death, my mother was already living with her maternal grandparents and their daughter, Aida. Divorced, impoverished, and with painfully severe arthritis, my grandmother Luisa supposedly fell off a second-floor balcony and was pronounced dead. Her death was considered an accident but I have always had my suspicions. As a child, my mother shared her letters with me, and Luisa always seemed sad.

Aida was the youngest of my great grandparents' children and therefore closer to my mother in age than her other aunts. My mother and Aida remained intimate throughout my mother's life. My mother's brother Isaac—nicknamed Chicho—went to live with his father. Unable to handle the boy, my maternal grandfather Israel sent Isaac to a fashionable Catholic school to teach the boy manners, but Isaac did not last there either. Israel owned race horses which presumably brought in enough money to allow him to pay for my uncle's privileged education. A picture shows my grandfather holding me with pride when I was a baby. He was well dressed, portly and wore a large Fedora. As a child, I was amazed and impressed that my grandfather owned beautiful horses. I was six when he died.

My mother's grandparents owned a women's hat shop in Cordoba. When it was closed, my female cousins and I were allowed to play with the hats that were considered unsellable. We pretended to be either saleswomen, or elegant customers trying on the grand hats with their ornaments of feather and tulle. The family lived behind the shop in rooms that led out to a central, long patio, the scene of large gatherings. I'm told that a small hut or "sukkah" had been built there in order to celebrate the holiday of Succoth but I never got to see it. Unlike my father's father, my mother's grandfather Joseph was a distinguished member of the Cordoba Jewish community. With his large, white mustache and well-trimmed beard, Joseph was a commanding presence, and yet he was always tender and playful with the great-grandchildren—and apparently tolerant since most of his children preferred a secular outlook to a religious one. All the men and Aida, Joseph's youngest daughter, became professionals. The rich intellectual atmosphere of the family had its effect on my mother as well.

In spite of not having finished high school by the time she married my father, my mother encouraged me to read and study rather than to emulate her excellent homemaking skills. She provided books and shelves on which to store them. Among my favorites were: *Aesop's Fables*, *Treasure Island* by Robert Louis Stevenson, *Far Away and Long Ago* by W.A. Hudson, *Twenty Thousand Leagues Under the Sea* by Jules Verne, and a number of novels by the well-known Spanish writer, Perez Galdos. My mother may have devoted herself to the care of my father, myself and my younger brother, but she was determined that I, her oldest child and only daughter, be thoroughly educated in all fields. It was her goal that I be able to support myself and, unlike most women of her era, not be financially dependent on a husband.

In 1929, my father graduated from medical school. (His specialty was dermatology and venereal disease, which thanks to penicillin is now less urgent.) That year he and my mother married in Cordoba. They made an attractive couple. There was Abraham, young, handsome and blue eyed - his stance remarkably erect. And Eugenia—full-figured with dark hair and passionate dark eyes. Because of her dark complexion, she was often affectionately known as "Negra," a term without negative connotations in Latin America. Happy, vivacious and with an easy laugh, she was the center of attention at any party.

Both Jews, my parents had a Jewish wedding, but they did not maintain a religious home. Their friends included, but weren't limited to the Jewish community in Buenos Aires. My father did not go to synagogue but he was deeply conscious of his ancestry and his religion. In 1936, for example, a group of fascist "brown shirts" attacked Jews in the street of Buenos Aires. With a friend, my father was ready to confront them. Years later during a WWII incident, he stole out at night to erase anti-Semitic graffiti.

I was born in Buenos Aires on February 23, 1930. (I led a privileged life. Up through the age of 12, I was cared for by two loving parents who encouraged my cultural interests.) A few months after my birth, we moved to a small town called Arias in the province of Cordoba. There, my father realized that the life of a general practitioner did not suit him. In later years, he confessed that he could not bear the sight of a sick child.

After a brief six months in Cordoba, we moved back to Buenos Aires. (At that time, my father received credentials certifying him as a "police doctor," a document that later became useful to him during the Perónist years when you could not renew your driver's license or obtain other documents without a "Certificate of Good Behavior," denied to those who did not sympathize with the government. Nobody else drove in the family. My father, old fashioned in his way, believed women should neither drive nor smoke. I didn't learn to drive until I came to the U.S.)

In Buenos Aires, our family shared a big house on Caseros Street with two of my father's siblings, my Uncle David and my Aunt Sophia. Caseros Street was a main road in Parque Patricios, the southern part of the city, paved with cobblestones and bordered by tall plantain trees. The house was historic – styled from a bygone era and predictably elegant. It was the site of some of my earliest memories. Also elegant was my Aunt Sophia, who had short, wavy black hair and dressed impeccably. She remained close to my parents all through my childhood and became our caretaker after my mother's death.

Stigol family, 1922

Standing left to right - Jose, Carlos, Elena, Catalina, Sonia's husband, Sofia, Sonia, David, Israel **Sitting left to right**: Raquel, Max, Abraham Rubin-Sophia's husband. Clara is reclined on her mother's lap. Toddler is Fanny Rudman, Sonia's elder daughter. Abraham is sitting holding baby Gregory, Fanny's brother.

Two incidents stand out from those early years. One occurred when my father was late in picking me up from the French kindergarten I attended. Waiting at the door, bereft that my classmates had already left, I sobbed uncontrollably, fearing I'd been abandoned. Years later, as a doctor picking up my own child after school, I realized how difficult it must have been for him to leave his office exactly on time. But how long those minutes seemed from my perspective as a child. I also remember, even at that young age, taking more than a little notice of a nice-looking boy in my class. Because I was only four, my parents found my ardor amusing. (Later, I realized that looks were my main priority in choosing male companions and saw that as a serious flaw.)

At four, my education included rigorous ballet lessons. Some of the exercises proved too strenuous for an eight-year-old, so I transferred to an academy where classes were less demanding. The old Russian master in charge was short and sturdy, like the one in some Degas paintings. Ballet classes meant more time with my mother who made my costumes and took pride in my success. At nine, modern dance lessons were added to my schedule. My new teacher, Otto Werber, was formerly of the famous Austrian Joos ballet, recently disbanded due to the Nazi invasion. The teacher chose me as the only student to participate in his solo dance performance of the *Pavanne Pour Une Enfant Defunte* by Ravel. It was the high point of my dance studies. Wrapped in a black cape that covered his body and half of his face (in contrast with the other half, which was chalky white), Otto personified death. Dressed in light blue and with my hair sprinkled with gold dust, I portrayed the dying princess. At age nine, I knew the thrill of being blinded by lights as I walked on stage, knowing that beyond the darkness an audience waited. Quite carried away with myself, I felt certain I was on the threshold of an artistic career. Unfortunately, my time with Otto was cut short by my parents who didn't take kindly to the fact that Otto's real life proclivities included a penchant for men.

One morning when I was six, I walked into my mother's room only to find her with my new brother Augusto in her arms. Eight days later I was relegated to the kitchen with our maid while the celebratory "briss" occurred. All I could hear from my perch was the baby's non-stop screaming. I feared for him, completely ignorant of what was happening. (As a pediatrician, I later questioned the need for circumcision unless done for ritual reasons. Medical research is still looking for a definite answer as to whether this procedure is capable of providing any protection from sexually transmitted diseases, a belief held by my father.)

During Augusto's first year of life, my treasured Shirley Temple doll was replaced by a baby doll so that I could imitate my mother as she cared for him. Still, I wondered about the need for this additional real baby who kept her busy and me jealous. When my brother was 14 months, an incident occurred that changed my feelings about Augusto and I felt closer to him. I was in the bathroom when he came crawling in, climbed up, and fell into a full bathtub. I quickly pulled him out and screamed for my mother as Augusto struggled to breathe. When he started to cry again, I realized he was saved. I also realized then that I did love him in some primal way. It lessened my displeasure at having to share him with my parents.

In 1936, I began first grade at a local public school, but an epidemic of poliomyelitis (polio) ended my attendance when my parents took me out of school. How much nicer it was to stay in my cozy home with my mother and baby brother. A year later, however, my formal education resumed - this time at the "Sarmiento" School on Callao Street in downtown Buenos Aires. I was admitted to the more advanced of the two available first grades. Sarmiento, the president of Argentina from 1868 to 1874, strongly believed in the power of education. He had recruited six teachers in Boston, Massachusetts, brought them to Buenos Aires, and under their direction, founded schools for women to be trained as teachers. These institutes retained their prestige throughout the time that I studied at them. In first grade, I won a spelling competition, which pleased my teachers, my parents and myself. It was the hopeful start of my academic future.

I had a new friend, too, Therese, and that added to the pleasure of attending school. One day, however, we were separated. While Therese remained with the rest of the class for a unit on "Religion," i.e., Catholicism, I and four other students were removed from the room. A Protestant, a Shintoist and two Jewesses like myself, were led to an empty classroom to hear a mishmash of words about "morals," suggesting that our parents had not properly addressed these matters. The real intent was to single us out as minorities. In this way I learnt that my father's respect for diverse spiritual orientations was not a value I would routinely encounter.

My family moved for a short summer sojourn to a northern suburb of Buenos Aires called Vicente Lopez. Supposedly, the fresher air would lessen the fierce attacks of whooping cough from which my brother and I suffered. It didn't, but we had fun. Having tasted and enjoyed the pleasant life of that quieter suburb, my parents decided to leave their apartment in the heart of Buenos Aires and to rent the ground floor of a two-family house with a garden in Vicente Lopez. My father commuted daily to his downtown office and drove me to school. I cherished those trips with him, the two of us talking or singing, even though the right pitch proved a mystery to both of us.

In the following year, 1939, my parents moved me from my beloved Sarmiento school to a local one much closer to our new flat. A child, I was, of course, not consulted. The new school occupied an old, unappealing building. After a brief test on the first day, I was promoted from third to fourth grade (a testament to the advanced classes at my previous school). My transition was facilitated by a kind and sensitive fourth grade teacher, and I continued to be at the top of the class with little effort. My continuing ballet lessons with the Russian teacher were the only link to my past. After the usual initial hesitations, my new classmates accepted my presence. Nonetheless, my old friendships from the Sarmiento could not be replaced.

While adjusting to the new school, I faced another unexpected event: the first separation from my parents. My father and his elder brother Joseph had an attachment almost as strong as that of a father and son. If Joseph needed support, Abraham would not ignore his call. In response to one of his marriage crises, my parents went to Cordoba for three days to support him. Augusto and I remained with a maid and our Aunt Sophia. To console me, my mother promised a special gift, and she came back with three paperbacks whose humble appearance disappointed me. I loved books and wouldn't have minded one with beautiful illustrations to add to my collection. The ones she brought me were printed on cheap paper, were easy to rip, and had strange titles: *Cabeza Rapada* (Shaved Head) and *Barcos de Papel* (Paper Ships) by Alvaro Yunque – a pseudonym (Yunque means anvil). Once I began to read one of them, however, I was entranced. *Cabeza Rapada* was about an eight-year-old orphan whose head was shaved to keep him free of lice and who earned his food cleaning floors. *Barcos de Papel* concerned a girl whose jealousy for her sibling was overcome when that sibling's face was mercilessly disfigured by small pox, a disease that was still prevalent in many parts of the world. Reading about lives so remote from my own pampered existence stirred undiscovered emotions. As the author lived near our home, I was able to obtain his signature which appears alongside one from my mother – with her praise for my good grades. I still keep this treasure with its signatures and comments.

News from the nonfictional world reached me through my father's comments about the European conflicts - the Spanish Civil War and the events that led up to World War II. My knowledge of these affairs depended solely on the comments of the adults around me, as there was no television to expose me to the horrors children routinely see today.

The year 1941 began auspiciously. I was eleven, in fifth grade, and encouraged by a superior teacher, I started to truly understand the process of learning. A skilled dancer, I helped the school raise funds which added to my popularity. At the same time, my mother began to experience vague abdominal pains. No one was able to diagnose her, and we went on with our plans to spend the December holidays with family in Cordoba.

The trip, over unpaved portions of road, always frightened me, but in the end it was worthwhile. I loved the time I spent with my dear cousins Annie and Luisa. On New Year's Eve I was ready to celebrate with my parents and our large extended family only to discover that at midnight, my father was absent. Recurring family crises had called him away to stay with my Uncle Joseph. The New Year, 1942, rang in without him. I felt his absence as a bad omen. My lasting memory of this trip is of my mother standing in front of my cousin Luisa's closet, organizing her clothes with one hand and holding a bag with hot water on her belly to control her pains. Later, when I became a doctor, I better understood the excruciating nature of the pains she suffered.

In February 1942, we attempted another joyous vacation at the seashore. Through my father's efforts, we were able to stay in three large tents facing the sea, outside of Mar del Plata, an elegant resort 240 miles south of Buenos Aires. My Uncle David's wife, Rebecca, and their daughters joined us. For a short period, the vacation was idyllic. We had a maid, the food was excellent, and the high class casino nearby was a source of fun and fashion for the adults. Soon, however, my mother's abdominal pains became too great for her to bear and we ended our vacation. Back in Buenos Aires, doctors did exploratory surgery to diagnose the origin of her symptoms (today's diagnostic methods did not exist). Both my father and his brother David were present when the skilled surgeon closed my mother's abdominal wound without any attempt to intervene: her pancreatic cancer was inoperable.

I went to see her often while she was in the hospital. One day I was shocked to see red blood in a draining bottle attached to her bed. Noticing my horrified expression, my mother explained that the fluids were merely the accumulated lipstick she had swallowed. After she was discharged, the surgeon visited her several times, a courtesy unheard of today. Nothing was said to me about the results of the operation – it was common in that era to hide the truth from children – but evidence of the seriousness of her illness seeped out. The first major sign of my new reality was the arrival of my aunts, Rebecca and Sophia, who had come to help pack our belongings and prepare us to leave our beautiful house in Vicente Lopez. I stood watching them fill boxes, not knowing where the boxes would go or when I would get my belongings back. My childhood was also packed away in those boxes.

A couple of years before my mother's illness, my father and his brother David, with the help of Joseph, had bought a Palladian-style house in the heart of the downtown section – on Montevideo Street, near Corrientes Avenue. The first floor was occupied by my father's medical practice, and a handsome reception hall led to his examining rooms. My Uncle David and his family lived upstairs. A broad oak staircase and a narrow elevator connected the two floors. I did not understand how generous my uncle and his wife were in letting us share space in their beautiful home, allowing us to insert our tragedy into their daily lives.

Lying there, my mother grew greener as the days passed. Downstairs, my father continued his practice, interrupted by and attending to my mother's intermittent cries of pain. In the back, on the second floor patio, my brother and our two cousins played, thrilled to have long hours together for their imaginary adventures. I slept on a cot in a corner of the children's bedroom and was told to use the "personnel" bathroom in the mezzanine on the back stairs. I look back with sadness at the humiliation this made me feel - including the fact that I was expected to dry the floor of the bathroom after showering (the tub lacked curtains). I felt ashamed and was perhaps too young – or preoccupied with events around me – to consider that there was only one other bathroom for both families. Perhaps I also sensed discomfort from those whose limited quarters I'd intruded into - even as they worried about my mother's fate.

The drastic change in my life conditions and the end of the ongoing dialogue I'd had with my parents, left me perplexed, and no one had time to help me sort out my confusion. Several times a day I put down my homework and went to see my mother. I was told that she was slowly recovering and it seemed natural to me that she would continue to attend to my needs. During one of those brief visits, my mother turned to my Aunt Sophia to ask for scissors. The day nurse held my mother so she could sit and trim my hair as she had always done. After my mother finished, my Aunt Sophia gathered the snipped hair ends and as I was leaving the room, told me to save them.

"Will my mother not be able to take care of me anymore?" was a question that crossed my mind, but I quickly rejected that unbearable thought.

After another of those brief visits, I noticed how much thinner her arms were and how green her complexion was. As I crossed the corridor

11

to go back to the family room, I stopped and looked downstairs over the veranda. I saw my father in his white gown crossing from one examining room to the other; I heard my brother playing with his cousins. The thought that my mother might die assaulted me. I could not imagine our lives without my mother's embracing love. If my mother were to die, I decided, then we needed to die too. First, my father would die, then my brother, and then I too would die.

I had to change schools once again. I was sent to a prestigious public school to complete sixth grade - the last year of primary school. Unlike in my two previous schools, I was assigned to the row of slow students – the justification given was that I had come from a less progressive suburban school. Unfortunately, the new teacher liked to shout at and humiliate the students in our row. She was nice only to Vera, an intelligent girl who was tall, blond and soft spoken. Vera had good manners and smiled at me my first day.

I found myself without a secure refuge either at home or school. My teacher was cruel, and my mother was dying. Despite the severity of my mother's condition, she grasped my anguish at the change from being the teacher's pet to one in the "dumb row." From her death bed, she managed to find an intelligent private tutor to help me. At the first semester exams, despite having been absent for the initial weeks, I scored as high as the best student in the class. As a result, I was taken out of the "dumb row" and the teacher shouted at me less. Vera and I became best friends.

I did my homework at Vera's house, spending afternoons enjoying her mother's hospitality. (Many years later, after losing contact, we met again when I was called to attend a delivery by an obstetrician friend. Ultrasounds and neonatologists did not exist, and the obstetrician had noticed problems in the fetus by his tacts and wanted to have a pediatrician supporting him. My heart broke when I arrived and realized the newborn was Vera's baby. She lost her child, and I continued to support her in whatever way I could during the following days.)

On a cold winter day in 1942, my thoughts turned to a constellation of issues: to the inclement winter weather, the overwhelming pain of my mother's illness and globally, to the horrid advance of Hitler's armies through Europe. I felt that this might be the most oppressive moment that I would ever experience.

On July 26, 1942, three months after her futile surgery - my mother died. I was 12 years old. Family members, hiding their distress, took my brother, our two cousins, and me to our Uncle Carlos' home. His kind wife included the four of us in her children's routine. I realized that something important had happened, but I preferred not to know what. I ignored the arrival of my Aunts Rebecca and Sophia on the following day and avoided their sad faces. My father came the day after to take us back to Uncle David's home; while he drove, he exhibited his usual interest in and tenderness towards each one of us. After entering the house, I walked upstairs and turned with hesitation towards my parents' room. It was dark. I understood then that the worst had happened. My father took me into the bathroom and breaking into the deepest sobs, told me that my mother had died. It was an agonizing moment for both of us. He told my brother, who was six, that she had merely gone to a hospital. Augusto learned of her death a year later from a classmate.

That night, I saw my father sleeping in a cot in his brother's bedroom. He looked to me like a refugee who had lost everything. Our lives had been shattered and we needed to pick up the pieces and go on.

For ten years after she died, my father mourned. He wore a black tie every single day. My mother had venerated my father, totally dedicating her life to him – and to us. When she died, he found it all but unbearable. He had spent devastating months watching her die, unable to help except for morphine shots he administered to decrease her suffering. I can still see him running upstairs in between patients to care for her.

Still, and perhaps because he had to be, my father was strong. He approached life as a rock pounded by waves.

"Life will try to knock you down, but you stand firm and remain yourself," he would advise me.

I learned from his words and from his example.

Somehow, he found the emotional energy to pick up and move on. He rented a small and sunny apartment around the corner from his office and resettled us there. My Aunt Sophia, who loved my father dearly and had loved my mother too, left her comfortable widow's life to come and care for us and help us survive as a family.

Despite my loss, I finished the 6th grade successfully, and even earned a first prize on a writing contest, with the help of my father's suggestions. For the rest of my life, studying would be my refuge. My beloved ballet lessons on the other hand, proved intolerable. I could no longer bear to witness other students with their mothers, a reminder of what I'd lost. In later years, wandering through the High Museum in Atlanta, I saw a painting by Degas that stirred strong emotions in me. A copy now hangs next to my desk. Its subject: two ballet students getting ready to dance with their mothers in the background, watching.

My mother's biggest legacy was my passion for books and for learning. I'd lost a lot in having to grow into womanhood without her. At the same time, my father's sensitivity enabled him to be a wonderful father as well as a best friend. Many of my interests for the rest of my life were modeled after his.

2

Teen Years and Medical School

I started my thirteenth year with the loss of my mother weighing heavily upon me. No wonder I failed to develop a sense of humor. Instead, I sought serious entertainment, the kind that could appeal to my feelings through artistic or intellectual means. Years later, my father-in-law, Hellmuth Weissenborn, an artist born in Germany, taught me the motto of the University of Leipzig: *Res severa est vera gaudium* (Only Serious Matters Give Real Pleasure). The statement was apt for his life and for mine.

Unlike American teenagers at the time, those from middle-class Argentine families were not terribly sports-oriented. And sports opportunities for most children were limited to the Young Men's Christian Association or to exclusive private clubs, beyond our financial reach, and certainly not available to Jews. My inclination to read and study limited my social opportunities as well. At thirteen, I carried a few extra pounds, wore glasses and braces, and had acne. I failed in my few attempts to learn social dancing and did not participate in the teen dances that took place in private homes. My refuge, therefore, was literature, my studies, and my second cousin Aida. Three years older than me and living close by, Aida was intelligent and grossly overweight. Ignored by boys, we turned our attention to cultural affairs, and since the year was 1943, to international matters related to World War II. Soon, a coup in our own country would also command our thoughts. My father's deep interest in and preoccupation with political events strongly contributed to my awareness of national and international conflicts.

In spite of the uneasiness created by my mother's death and the political climate, my father somehow found ways to brighten my life. With money he gave me, I purchased two subscriptions so that my cousin and I could listen to Beethoven's nine symphonies at the legendary Colon Theater. I still remember the excitement of going by myself to buy the tickets. Up until this point, music had merely been background for dance; it had a narrative. After these visits, it became an abstract world in which I delighted and would never leave. The opposite seasons between the northern and southern hemispheres permitted the greatest musicians and opera singers to visit Argentina during the European and American summer recess.

We had the privilege of listening to the renowned Fritz Busch and Eric Kleiber conducting Beethoven. I became conscious then of my father's infinite generosity and the impact it had upon my life. He continued showering me with such priceless gifts until his progressive blindness slowed him down in later years.

In 1943, the Soviet and German armies were locked in a deadly fight; the Allies had invaded Sicily. The future of our world was at stake. At home, on June 4 of that year, a coup by the Argentine army ended with a constitutional government headed by a weak vice-president. The military's intention was to align the country with the Axis (Germany, Italy and Japan) against the Allies (England, France and Russia). Juan Domingo Perón, merely a colonel at the time, was installed in a new Department of Work and Social Protection *(Prevision Social),* where he spewed his demagogic propaganda. He had gone to Europe and had trained in the footsteps of Mussolini. This was not the country's only flirtation with fascism.

General Jose Felix Uriburu had also taken power by a coup in 1930. In 1943, however, fascists in Europe were more organized and refined in their methods. My experiences under the 1943 military government – even then – planted the seeds of my desire to emigrate. A painting that currently hangs in my dining room by the gifted artist Manuel Kantor illustrates that longing: a Bahiana sitting on a deck in the harbor, gazing at the departing boats and their sails. The picture reminds me of my own desire, upon seeing those ships, to leave the authoritarian regime of my birthplace for more enlightened lands. Eventually, I did.

In 1943, bookshops in Buenos Aires were so small that it was not unlikely for an owner to have read his entire inventory and to advise customers on which books they might prefer. One often met well-known writers and politicians in these shops. Reading the owner's recommendations at one of these shops which I frequented increased my awareness of not only history and current events but of art as well. My father was the good friend with whom I shared my discoveries.

In 1943, I began high school. In Argentina, it consisted of five years of baccalaureate study, after which a student would choose to go on for a graduate degree at the University. There was only a state university which was public and free. (It wasn't until 1956 that private universities were created.) I applied to the Sarmiento High School, where I had attended the first three grades of elementary school. To help me prepare for the difficult entrance exam, my father hired the same tutor my mother had selected during her illness.

There were times when my dear father was not fully able to substitute for my lack of a mother. For example, I had issues with the silk stockings I wore for the first time during my high school entrance examination. They kept falling and embarrassing me. Although physically awkward, I was agile mentally and that gave me an advantage.

After passing the entrance test to the new school, I became reacquainted with Gilda, a girl I had known earlier. Gilda belonged to a sophisticated, hospitable family. Her father, considerably older than her mother, had been one of the idealistic Russians involved in early attempts to end Czarist rule. Gilda and I spent long hours together studying and discussing the major political and philosophical problems of the world. There was no question in our minds that even as girls, we deserved the same opportunities as boys and men. (We both eventually became physicians.)

The dictatorship under which we lived colored my high school years. Our history teacher, for example, was a young lawyer who believed in a constitutional government and also taught us about government in ancient Greece. We respected him more because of it. Since he was young, we were all in love with him as well. I was proud to be one of his best students, and he appreciated the serious attitude with which I approached my work. Many years later, in 1999, I went with my family to the Acropolis in Athens. The guide was surprised by how much Greek history I remembered. My fascination with what I learned in those history classes stayed with me.

Another of my high school teachers had a vivacious and daring personality. A favorite, despite her declared sympathy for the regime, she believed the economically disadvantaged would be rescued by the current government. It was she who recommended one of several important books that influenced my adolescence, *Daughter of Earth*, an autobiographical novel by Agnes Smedley. An early champion of women's rights and birth control, Smedley was rediscovered by the women's movement in America in the 1980s. Another distinctive quality of the pro-Perónist teacher was that she lived with a man, but we weren't sure whether they were married. We found that quite fascinating.

My math teacher also stood out; the author of the math books we were required to read. Higher level studies after medical school, however, did not confirm that my math skills were adequate, and I was left feeling rather inept. (If I'd known that one day my eldest daughter would be a distinguished statistician, I might have felt better.)

My one clear failure was in music class. I could not – and still cannot – sing a note. One day the music teacher decided that she also had a responsibility to those who had not been selected for the choir. She asked three of us to go to the front of the class and attempted to teach us. After a very short while, she sent us back to our seats, saying that listening to us was simply unbearable. And yet, the joy of hearing the human voice at its best remains one of my passions.

When I was fifteen and in what would correspond to the tenth grade in America, I felt the need to oppose the authoritarian regime, and I tried to sell tickets to a political function. The new headmistress took me aside and asked me to stop; otherwise, she explained, she'd have to suspend me from school which she was loath to do since I was one of her best students. Many of us felt we were living a double life. We tried to behave as obedient students but secretly we strongly resented the regulations imposed on us by the fascist-leaning government.

I felt deeply in conflict. Like any adolescent, I reevaluated those around me. I realized that even my beloved father was far from perfect. Occasionally he would forget something he had promised. He was also casual about how he spent money (even though he worked so hard that money was not a problem).

At 13, I was extremely independent and had to find my own way. The enchantment of being a woman, of adorning myself, was lost to me. Without a mother to guide me, I didn't wear a bra or lipstick until I was 21. I was troubled by my developing breasts which embarrassed me. I was often tired and wondered if I was sick. Life seemed intense and so uneven. Some days I was enthusiastic, other days sad. Even minor daily troubles affected me disproportionately. "Why all these ups and downs?" I wondered. The answer and at least some enlightenment came in the form of a thin book given to me by my great-aunt Eugenia (my mother's aunt), a cultured and progressive person. The book, *The Ambition and Anguish of Adolescents*, by Anibal Ponce, explained the changes in my body and their effect on my mind. Ponce was part of a group of very progressive psychologists whose approach was antithetical to the more repressed approach prevalent in a Catholic country. His book, which linked changes in physiology to changes in psychology, was perceived as radical. Bodily changes in adolescents were simply not discussed. Had my mother been alive, I might have had at least an inkling of the importance of these changes. Luckily for me, however, I was in contact with some open-minded people. I saw that the feelings I had were not unusual; they were simply the result of being an adolescent.

The military coup d'etat that installed a Fascist government in Argentina and Perón's presidencies lasted from my first year of high school, 1943, for 12 years, until 1955. Unlike in the US, students did not have four years of college to decide on a career. Therefore, at the age of 16, I had to choose a career; I chose medicine. Some of the reasons for my choice are obvious. My father was a doctor; his experiences were inspiring, and medicine is a profession that I could practice anywhere. This was important since already I had dreams of emigrating to a country that offered greater freedom. But to my surprise, when my father learned of my decision to study medicine, he was not pleased.

"My dear daughter," he said, "medicine is not for a woman. You will not be able to take care of your husband and your children."

I did not argue with him, but during the fifth and last year of high school, I studied for the entrance examination anyway.

How large the corridors seemed when I went to take the admissions test. And how small, I, a teenager, felt. Just taking the test made me feel as if I'd left my adolescence behind. My dear cousin Gregory, who wanted to be a dentist, took the exam at the same time and failed. It made me even more aware of the big step I was taking.

The year I took the exam was intense for other reasons. Meetings among students were forbidden, but we found a way to gather, discuss the political situation, and lament the quality of our teachers – all while preparing a play to be performed at our graduation. A few days after my high school graduation in December 1946, I passed the entrance examination to medical school. Faced with the facts, my father became a main supporter of my career.

I rested for three months at the then elegant ocean resort of Mar del Plata and in March 1947, began the first year of medical school. The entire year was devoted to a course called "Descriptive Human Anatomy." We used the same French books written by Leo Testut, the renowned French physician, that my father had used. I memorized every detail of each bone in the human body, knowledge that I rarely used in later years. I performed human dissections using the same metal box and tools my father had used as well. We studied muscles, tendons, vessels, nerves, and the more accessible organs in cadavers, never losing a sense of respect for the corpse. When we finished, we stitched them back up as if they had not been touched.

Anatomy was taught as it had been for centuries, without much consideration for the function of the structures whose parts we had to so scrupulously memorize. I got an A on the final exam and went back to the seaside. Those two boundless and carefree summers near the sea were special. I loved the ocean – its power, its immensity – and I loved how the scenery constantly changed with shifts in the light or wind. A poem by Baudelaire called *The Man and the Sea* expresses the sense of wonder the sea inspires.

> Free man! the sea is to thee ever dear!
> The sea is thy mirror, thou regardest thy soul
> In its mighteous waves that unendingly roll,
> And thy spirit is yet not a chasm less drear.

In addition to my studies, 1947 was rich with experiences. Poly, (short for Leopold), was one of my classmates. He was a member of a select group that had graduated from one of the best high schools in the country, known informally as the "Buenos Aires" (since many of its students went on to the University of Buenos Aires). These students came from a cultured background and considered themselves existentialists, a movement about which I knew little.

Buenos Aires had many cafes in which you could nurse a demitasse for hours. We had long conversations in these cozy rooms. I was constantly challenged about my supposedly simplistic, leftist and idealistic vision of the world. Those were the "cold war" years between Russia and United States. The Soviets had conducted one of the most extensive public relations campaigns ever, and I was influenced by it too. Living in a country with so many socio-economically deprived people, it was logical that Marxist ideas would appeal to our young, idealistic minds. The reality was hidden.

I decided to free myself from personal ties that could limit me, so I broke up with the young man I had been dating. A typical adolescent, he overreacted and threatened suicide. He soon abandoned the idea and replaced me with another medical student - prettier and wealthier than I - whom he eventually married. With my new, hipper friends, I explored art and politics. I attended operas and concerts with Poly, whose father was the musical critic for *La Prensa*, the most prestigious newspaper in Argentina. Also significant in our group was Ernesto Deira, who became a famous painter and Allan Poe Castelnuovo, the son of a well-known writer. A nephew of the painter Spilimbergo was also in the group.

That same year, a renowned psychiatrist, Gregorio Bermann, used my father's office to see his Buenos Aires patients. As a kind gesture to my father, he invited me to visit his family and clinic in Cordoba. I had relatives in that city, an additional reason for going, and I accepted his offer. He lived with his daughter Silvia in a small house called The Refuge, next to his clinic. The clinic was housed in a large and old mansion surrounded by a park. The more modest Refuge was quiet and conducive to study and intellectual work. I loved the environment for other reasons as well; it was free from the distractions of my younger brother and my darling Aunt Sophia, who was getting on my nerves. Sophie had taken care of my mother and had devoted herself to us, but she was obsessively neat, a fact that as a teenager, I could not tolerate.

A few weeks after my visit to the Bermann home, I attended a talk in Buenos Aires given by my former host. There I met his son Claudio. Tall and swarthy, he looked very attractive in his soldier's uniform - he was completing the obligatory draft period. I imagined the Arab blood of his maternal ancestors who came from Spain, the Barrancos, running through him. Everything about him charmed me – his voice, his lips, through which he exhaled round, even circles of cigarette smoke. From the first meeting, I could think only about when I might see him next. I decided that the other young men I'd dated, merely inspired friendship. What was stirring in me now felt different. Was it love?

In 1948, during the second year of medical school, I examined under a microscope the same organs and structures that I had studied the previous year in cadavers and had observed preserved in formaldehyde.

Finished with his year of service, Claudio had returned to his family's home in Cordoba. Even before my classes started, I received an invitation to attend a wedding in that city. I was certain that I would see him there. I ordered a custom-made décolleté white blouse and a dark brown, bell-shaped skirt that went way beyond the knee - the first to be seen in that provincial town. Claudio attended the wedding and looked even more handsome in a white suit that contrasted to stunning effect with his dark skin. We talked and we danced, and when the evening was over, he drove me to my aunt's place where I was staying. The next day my aunt insisted on taking me and my cousin Luisa to the mountains. I was crushed. I only wanted to stay home and wait for Claudio to call. As it happened, I got sick, which forced an end to our outing. When we returned, Claudio called to invite me to dinner. After dinner, he took me for a ride to Sarmiento Park. Our first kiss fed my romantic expectations. It was the first time I'd experienced a strong physical attraction to a man.

Happily, Claudio had plans to move to Buenos Aires, where we saw each other frequently. I continued to be charmed by his worldly manners and appearance, and I was convinced that the strong feelings I harbored were an expression of a deep and lasting love. A few weeks after his arrival in Buenos Aires, we surprised my father at the dinner table by wearing engagement rings. My father first noticed Claudio's ring, and knowing that I was interested in him, quietly lamented the fact that he was already engaged, presumably to someone else. Only later did my father notice a similar ring on my finger. Everyone rejoiced. Our rings were inscribed with the date 5-8-1948, which had significance for us. We'd read in the news that the British Record on Partition was submitted to a Special Session of the General Assembly of United Nations on May 8 which initially we considered the original birth date of Israel. Now, of course, Israel's birth date is considered May 14th. (We didn't suspect the conflicts that would arise from the Partition.) So the May 8 date seemed like a good omen.

My future father-in-law, approving his son's choice, invited us to the renowned Richmond Café (which remained open until 2011). My father, always worrying about the vacuum left by my mother's death, believed that the marriage would be a chance for me to find the happiness he had always wished for me. With his usual generosity, he was prepared to cover most of our financial needs. My future father-in-law also pledged to help. Having witnessed my parents' loving marriage, I had a positive model for married life, and so, happily and with little angst, I prepared to take this next step. Both fathers supported our decision to marry soon. I was also eager for the engagement to be short. The concept of the fallen woman – one who had sex before marriage – was still prevalent in Argentina in the mid-twentieth century, and being a young woman of my time, I adhered to that notion. At the same time, I was mightily attracted to Claudio and was eager to enjoy the intimacy marriage entailed.

The three months between our engagement and our wedding passed as if in a dream. While a designer finished a light blue dress for me – I did not want anything as traditional as a white dress – I shopped with a friend in an elegant lingerie shop for a few post-wedding essentials. The salesperson ignored me at first, apparently assuming I was too young to be a bride (I was 18; Claudio was 22). When I went to ask my doctor to be a witness at our civil ceremony, he congratulated me for the choice of family I was planning to marry into but cautioned me about the short engagement period. He was the only one who raised that issue. Our respective fathers were oblivious to the folly of a short engagement. Our courtship, which though intense, had only consumed the better part of three months – from when Claudio came to live in Buenos Aries in May of 1948 until our wedding on July 31. My fiancé's mother was teaching abroad and my own mother, of course, was no longer living.

So, after our hurried engagement, Claudio and I were married. We needed my father's signature to make the marriage official as I was legally still a minor. The wedding party was an elegant affair, held from seven to nine in the evening. The notables attending included the great Spanish poet, Rafael Alberti, a friend of my father-in-law.

I was not a typical American teenager who at 18 begins college and also begins to think about what she wants to be. I was married and already in the second year of medical school. My teen years were 13 to 17. I was a bride, yes, but at the same time, I was also a full-time second year medical student. Claudio abandoned his medical studies and became a poorly-paid journalist for a communist newspaper. As expected, we were financially dependent on my father, a fact that, for some strange reason, didn't raise objections from any quarter. In retrospect, I see how foolish and immature we were. I especially saw the world and our future two-dimensionally, without depth or complexity. To get married was to guarantee happiness, a myth that today, thank goodness, fewer women embrace.

The next step for us, all assumed, was to have children. When a few months went by and I did not get pregnant, I consulted a gynecologist. He explained that young women may not ovulate every month. The extent of my ignorance about sexual physiology would astound a young woman of today, especially one in medical school. (I was just starting to learn about it in school). My mother's absence and the taboo of sex in our society contributed to my ignorance. My aunt Sophia suggested that I talk to a friend: a divorcée, who she suspected knew about sex.

"What if I should wish to avoid a pregnancy?" I asked that friend.

She suggested the use of suppositories.

"Where do you insert them – front or back?" I asked.

In 1949, during my third year in medical school, I studied physics, chemistry and physiology. The final was a written multiple choice test including those subjects. I passed with a "B"; ten days later, on November 26, my first child was born.

The skillful obstetrician was my father-in-law's brother, who helped me have a natural delivery, giving birth to a baby girl with her father's black hair and black eyes. We named her Georgina. The first night at his private clinic after the delivery, with my baby and husband sleeping on either side of me, I stayed fully awake. Or was I in a trance? I assumed the life that would follow would be one of bliss – one that only the very young – and untested – might imagine. Luckily, summer arrived, and I was able to breastfeed my baby full time, a practice I continued part-time after my fourth-year classes began. My chubby baby was a source of happiness for the whole family.

Other areas of my life were less idyllic. Focused on my studies and my baby, I had put many old friendships aside. I also seemed to have lost the companionship of my husband. It was not until Georgina turned a year old that I realized how many responsibilities I was carrying and how lonely I felt at times facing them. Our somber political situation did not help either. We lived under a dictatorship that had the right to torture or eliminate the opposition, and that meant problems for Claudio which surfaced the night before Georgina's birth. Claudio had been told that he would assume responsibility for an article published by the communist newspaper where he worked. He didn't write it – one of the party leaders had – but the editors informed him that he could be jailed for it. On the eve of that first pregnancy, with my belly big, I had had to get rid of a suitcase full of books not approved by the government. A few hours later, I felt delivery pains.

In 1949, Hungary's new constitution alerted us to the realities of communism. I recognized that my opinions clashed with those of my husband and his circle. I doubted the utopia and better world promised under communism. My doubts grew about the regime in Russia, and I had trouble feeling solidarity with the Argentine communists. Initially, Argentine communists opposed Perón and as a consequence became alienated from the working class who fell for Perón *en mass*. Even though brutally persecuted during Perón's regime, the communists ultimately supported him. I did not share Claudio's enthusiasm for the communists and my sentiments affected our marriage.

When the Perón government closed the newspaper where Claudio worked, my husband was out of work. Even before his job loss, we'd had financial problems because we lived beyond our means.

Claudio was not earnestly looking for work. I was a full-time student. As a result, I found myself responsible for the house, the child and my career, while my father subsidized us. All signs pointed to the wisdom of avoiding a second pregnancy, but I was convinced that Georgina would have a fuller life with a sibling.

In 1950, in my fourth year of medical school, we were taught how to recognize signs of disease in hospitalized patients. Our eyes, ears and hands were our main tools to diagnose their ailments. X-rays and blood tests were requested after we'd made a tentative diagnosis, spending considerable time using thorough questionnaires and detailed physical exams.

In the long, rectangular in-patient wards of the teaching hospital, a large container of urine stood next to each bed. We based some of our conclusions on the amount, turbidity and color of that fluid, as well as on the foam that resulted after shaking the container. Then we sent the urine to the lab for confirmation. The patients asked us endless questions too. One of my patients was a man in his early forties with a very large spleen in his abdomen and larger than normal lymph nodes. Clearly he had Hodgkin's disease, for which there was inadequate treatment. Therefore, I did not discuss his prognosis with him, but I was developing empathy for him. His concern for his condition was dwarfed by his concern for the future of his wife and only child. I remember him so vividly.

I also recall my oral final examination that year. Professors, students and my own father watched me with pride, seeing how I had progressed as a medical student. During the examination, I explained how my diagnosis was based on traditional steps: observation, interrogation and physical examination. How proud to get an "A." In my pathology course, under a microscope, we examined abnormal cells and tissues from diseased whole organs preserved in formaldehyde. What we had done with so-called normal organs during our first and second years of study, we repeated now on diseased organs. Today tests can show and measure an organ, like the heart, and determine how well it functions. But when I studied medicine few of those tests were available. We relied on pathology, the study of the organs after death. Autopsies confirmed or changed our clinical diagnoses and were, therefore, important teaching exercises. During the fifth year of my career I studied surgery, pharmacology (the study of medications and their effects), bacteriology, and parasitology.

One day while performing routine bureaucratic duties at medical school, a clerk looked at my records and said, "Do you know that with your grades, you could apply to be an intern at the Hospital de Clinicas (the university hospital)?"

I hadn't dreamed I could be eligible. Training at the university hospital was, after all, an honor reserved for the best students. From that day on, I worked with even greater enthusiasm.

Applicants to the Hospital de Clinicas had to be approved by the residents corps, known for their ethnic and religious prejudices. Until a few years before I entered that hospital, for example, there were no Jewish residents. I was nervous when I went for my interview with the senior and junior residents under whom I would have to work. Solemnly they stood in the patio of the hospital, dressed in their white surgical suits and starched white coats. Their height and important appearance contrasted with my size and naiveté. As the interview went on, I relaxed and felt obliged to tell them that I might be pregnant again - with the consequent interruption of services that this would imply. Rumors had reached my interviewers that I was a Jew and had harbored leftist inclinations. But in this instance, my skepticism was not confirmed: they accepted me as their intern despite the strikes against me.

Of thirty-nine interns and residents, nine were women; I was the first female intern to work while pregnant. I did not refuse any task, and I worked the usual long hours. It was my first experience practicing medicine and my enthusiasm gave me the energy to cope with the long hours.

Thankfully I had help at home - at least in terms of childcare. Since Georgina's birth, I'd always had some kind of professional help. The first nanny was a young girl. When I tried to replace her with a more mature nanny, Georgina rebelled. Eventually we hired the faithful Cecilia, who remained with us through the birth of my second child. I relied mostly on my father for money. Claudio was without a job and his father helped, but not much. Had I not had my father to rely upon, I could not have remained in medical school.

I still remember my first patient as an intern – even all these years later. She was a young woman dying of an infection due to her attempt to abort a pregnancy. Unable to face the shame of being single and pregnant, or of wanting to abort her child, she died denying it. I was pregnant with my second child at the time and naturally her drama had a special resonance with me.

Another memory lingers of a patient from that era. I think of him at times when financial considerations are weighed against prolonging human life. In one of our evening rounds, in the large ward where patients were deposited after surgery, we saw a very old man whose leg had been amputated earlier in the day. He appeared to be in a coma. I was certain these were his last hours and that he did not need much care. How wrong I was. Two nights later I saw him sitting on his bed, smiling and expecting the promised visit of his son. Despite his difficulties, he appeared ready to face life again. Never again would I discount anyone's chance to survive.

I continued to learn, whether from studying for an exam or acquiring bedside experience. I managed to meet my responsibilities at work and at home. I was taught by my immediate junior and senior residents to deliver the best possible care, even if the means for doing so were limited – a commitment that stayed with me for the rest of my career.

The male residents lived in a separate building of the hospital. They had private rooms and their own food service. The few female medical residents had to sleep in the hospital during their nights on call in a room in a distant corner - far from the emergency room and the patients' wards. The room lacked shower facilities. Female residents in pharmacy were more numerous than in medicine and did not have overnight duties. I rarely had time to mingle with the pharmacy residents, but some of my male colleagues did. Some even married them.

To understand the Hospital de Clinicas, you need to know how medicine was practiced in Argentina at that time. Then (as now), a two-tier system of public and private hospitals. The ability to pay decided where patients went.

Public hospitals were free and responsible for the training of medical graduates. The Hospital de Clinicas, supported by the University of Buenos Aires, was also free, having opened to the public in 1881. The attending physicians were professors of the medical school. Interns and residents were chosen from the best students in each class. So being a resident at the Hospital de Clinicas was extremely prestigious, comparable to being a resident at a hospital associated with Columbia or Harvard.

Below the low arched front hallway were paths leading to one and two-story buildings painted yellow but darkened by city soot. Most of these buildings had been constructed according to old cannons and were similar to those I later saw in Florence. A few old trees, bushes and wooden benches remained in the otherwise barren garden surrounding the buildings. Winters are mild in Buenos Aires, and if the weather and a lull in our work permitted, we sat al fresco and philosophized about our mission. My memories returned to the many days and nights I walked along these various crossroads, either to the various hospital wings or, exhausted, to the isolated room where the women residents slept.

A specialty residence in pediatrics did not exist. We in the emergency room had to take care of both surgical and medical problems for patients of all ages. At the same time, we were in our last years of medical school and striving to learn useful techniques. Some residents were more savvy than others, having had family members who preceded them, and having trained and attained important positions at the hospital. The prestige of being a physician began to be established in those humble buildings. High standards in the practice of medicine were the pride of the old hospital, where nuns still played the administrative roles. Doctors received little or no pay for their morning work other than the prestige acquired from belonging to the staff and the opportunities that affiliation provided. After all, other hospitals funneled their most challenging cases to ours.

As residents, we were exposed to realities we had not confronted before in our pampered lives. We were challenged to deliver the best possible care to every patient, regardless of class or background - and without the incentive of financial remuneration.

One of the intern's duties was to give ether anesthesia to patients who were operated on in the emergency room - ether administered using an old leaky system. No one had knowledge of the effect on a fetus of those noxious gases, but fortunately one of my colleagues thought it was better to exclude me from performing that task. In general, however, my pregnant condition was overlooked at work until my belly grew too large to be ignored. My superiors, as gentlemen, felt embarrassed assigning me tasks in front of patients. Finally, one emergency room doctor ordered me to stop coming to work. My fellow interns had to replace me for the remaining days of my internship. I remain forever thankful to those who filled in for me. They sacrificed time that they needed to devote to their studies.

Meanwhile at home, our household – which consisted of the small staff I employed to help me run the house and care for my toddler - was in disarray. The cause was once again politics. A group of military men threatened to remove Perón from power, and as a result, he requested the solidarity of his followers. In September 1951, big crowds responded, culminating in a giant rally. My helpers left my home to demonstrate.

Feeling weak, I went to see my obstetrician. He decided that I needed more help than I was getting and suggested either that I enter his private hospital or, out of concern for my health, interrupt the pregnancy. Not mentioned was my husband's obvious absence from his responsibilities. Weary and distressed, I looked for a hotel with a kitchenette for Georgina and myself. She was one and one half years old, and I planned to move with her and the nanny. I was made aware by a lawyer friend, that taking this step I had to go to a "decent house" or I would face the threat of losing my children - and that a hotel did not meet those standards. I didn't know what to do. When my father learned of my circumstances, he insisted that Georgina and I move back into his home. There had been no offensive words between Claudio and me, but surprisingly, I felt relieved to leave. I knew now I would be well cared for.

Soon after I had moved in with my father, however, I was diagnosed with rubella and ordered to stay in bed for one week. I had picked up the illness working in the emergency room. The devastating effects of rubella in the unborn child were first described in 1942. It was1951, almost a decade later, yet I had still not been told about them. The only recommendation I received was to get bed rest. At that time, doctors protected their patients from worries and did not discuss painful possibilities with them.

Cared for by my Aunt Sophie, I felt better after a few days. Two months later, while standing on line to register to take an exam, a classmate asked why I hadn't been in class during the previous month. When she found out about my rubella, she said, "My mother had the same illness when she was pregnant and my sister was born with a bad heart." That's how I learned of the risks. I went to see my internist who, although well informed, said, "It is out of the question to interrupt your pregnancy at this point."

I was in my sixth month. Of course ultrasounds didn't exist and so I spent the next three months worrying about the child in my womb.

During the last two months of my pregnancy, it was very hot, and I needed relief. I took Georgina and her nanny to a modest, two-room apartment my father owned in what was then an elegant resort called Mar del Plata, 250 miles south of Buenos Aires. For my 22nd birthday, my mother-in-law, who'd always intrigued me with her natural elegance and strong personality, came to visit me. She brought my husband and was intent on reuniting Claudio and me. As an enticement, she brought me a charming antique watch. For whatever reason, my husband was also in a loving mood – paying me the attention I'd longed for – and by the end of the visit we decided I would return home and to him.

My worries about the health of my fetus were resolved happily. On March 30, 1952, I gave birth to Marcelo, a healthy, beautiful boy with blue eyes and his father's dark hair. I have never stopped being grateful for his good health. My relationship with Claudio, however, was not as healthy. During the week after Marcelo's birth which I spent in a private hospital, my father was the consistent male presence. He was present at my discharge. He took me home. He paid the bill.

Claudio's failure to step up and care for me and his children continued to strain our relationship. We tried to smooth our differences for the sake of our children, but they remained my responsibility with little help from Claudio. Finally we decided to separate. This time, however, it was my husband who agreed to leave the house. He moved to Cordoba to resume his medical studies, and afterwards we were officially divorced. For years I lived feeling as if had a "D" mark on my forehead - denouncing me as a divorcée. After all, I lived in a society where divorce was not as common or acceptable as it is today. Still, I managed. My children and my studies filled my life.

About a month and a half after Marcelo was born, I returned to work. Though at home I'd been able to breast feed him full time, when I returned to work I could only do so part time. Ironically, there was no place in the hospital environment where I could safely save my pumped milk, so it was not possible to nurse him after three months.

How much had happened in a mere three years. I'd gotten engaged, married, become pregnant – twice – and separated from my husband. Did these events and the tense political climate affect my studies? Undoubtedly. I had difficulty with my oral examinations and during my second to last year of medical school, my grades dropped. Was it due to a problem with memory, a lack of time to study, or to a loss of my ability to express myself? Who knows? As my grades slipped, the possibility of ending my training at the hospital became a depressing reality.

The "spirit of corps" dictated that I should stay. But every year there was a new selection of residents, and another candidate had applied to take my job. My colleagues discussed the possibility of accepting my replacement, a man named Felix who had evidently charmed them. It was decided that Felix and I would share my first year of residency. Soon, I, too, became charmed by Felix and his family who became some of my dearest lifetime friends. After Felix got married and after I graduated, his children were my first patients.

Intern at the Hospital de Clinicas

My medical class was supposed to graduate in December of 1953. A small number of us, however, for various reasons, graduated several months later. I graduated in May of 1954 with two beautiful children and my degree.

3

After Medical School, 1954-1965

A year after my graduation from medical school, I was a 24-year-old divorcée, living with Georgina, four, and Marcelo, two, in our spacious apartment in Buenos Aires. Our material needs were met, thanks to my father's unceasing support. I did not drive, which limited our outdoor and weekend activities. My father picked up the slack here, too. He took Marcelo along on his regular trips to his *quinta*, or little farm, which he'd bought when my brother was ten and I was sixteen, and which we all loved.

As my children grew, nannies became less useful. The children attended school from 8 a.m. to noon, near the hospital where I worked (and had trained) in the outpatient pediatric unit. I found an after-school program to guide them as they did their homework and introduce them to creative activities. It did neither but the children found the program entertaining and stayed.

I rode the subway with them to school, but meeting them for the ride home was challenging. I could not always be sure of arriving at their school on time. Returning home, they were hungry and tired, and not in the best of moods. Marcelo liked to sit in the first car of the train so he could watch as it entered the tunnel. Georgina liked to express her displeasure by tossing her school bag on the sidewalk every few steps on our way to and from the train, which provoked me and her brother.

After she finished sixth grade, Georgina passed a test to enter the prestigious high school connected with the University of Buenos Aires. Two years earlier, at age nine, she had declared that she would not study medicine because doctors, like me, knew only about their profession. They did not read Homer unabridged, for example, as she was doing even then. Marcelo attended first grade at a school near our house with several children from our building. After a few years, he and Roberto, one of his friends from this group, transferred to a private, bilingual school. Marcelo studied hard and became proficient in English. Eventually I became the pediatrician for that schoolmate and developed a lifelong friendship with his family.

Luisa with Georgina and Marcelo

During summers, Georgina and Marcelo vacationed at their father's home. In my lovely apartment, suddenly quiet, I listened to the wonderful music that is still broadcast in Buenos Aires, including sacred choral music at Christmas. I continued studying medicine even though my exams were over, believing that to be a good doctor, one never stops studying.

At the hospital, I was in charge of the infancy clinic and saw cases of severe malnutrition. I taught and completed my training by visiting different specialty departments established for adults as many were not yet organized exclusively for children. My position was important, and I worked hard, but I was not paid. Free for patients, the hospital was considered a training field for doctors - a prestigious place where we could sharpen our skills. Most doctors were paid little or nothing for their morning work, although in the afternoon they earned money in their private practices. It wasn't until 1955 that I finally started to earn some money by filling in for doctors on the weekends or when they were away on vacation. My father continued to support us. In fact I did not fully support my family until we emigrated to the United States in 1965.

For household support, I had a number of people to help with child-care and other activities. A few were wonderful, and I couldn't have functioned without them. Others were inadequate, and when I learned how they mistreated my children through neglect, abuse or indifference, I resented them bitterly. I concluded that occasionally encountering inferior childcare providers was an occupational hazard for any working parent.

Did my children resent the long hours I worked? Of course. And they expressed it in different ways. For one thing, they were displeased by the space I used for my office. It was hard for them to understand my efforts as a single mother, that I was trying to build a financial future for our family. I worked hard, always choosing jobs that would raise my professional status and eventually support us. My daughter was not interested in spending time with her brother. Marcelo often felt isolated from the two of us. Georgina, being older, could discuss subjects Marcelo was too young to understand. The relationship between the children was far from perfect, nor was the outcome of my attempts to juggle family life and work. Claudio lived in another town and was absent from their lives except for the months of the children's vacation.

Yet despite those challenges, we lived in an atmosphere of love and affection. The children brought joy and tenderness to my life. I tried to make life pleasant for them by being rational in my parenting techniques. I tried to explain my behavior to them. In some sense, that effort strengthened our relationship. Still, they contested my authority, and often I was too lenient. Only on a few occasions, when really frustrated, did I resort to methods I later regretted. Even though in theory I rejected spanking them, my words didn't always stop their unacceptable aggressive behaviors. In retrospect, I believe it is better if the parent establishes reasonable but firm limits, even if the reasons for those limits are not clear to the child. Explaining one's logic alone has its limitations.

My social life was curbed, naturally, as I needed time with my children, and I had to keep up with the fast pace of changes in medicine. What leisure time I had I spent visiting my father's family or the friends and relatives whose children I treated. There was never a man by my side. Since my social exposure was restricted, the hospital was the most likely place to meet someone. During my residency, I felt strongly attracted to one of my fellow residents. I spent a year and a half carefully hiding my feelings until he declared his own. He'd obtained a scholarship to go to France. I received some subsidy money to accompany him, but in the end I didn't go. Extremely loving in private, our relationship was never acknowledged in public. I thought it was time to get married, but I'd learned that his father had voiced objections to our relationship. Was his issue that I was a Jew and had two children? We painfully separated. This taught me not to expose my children to the men I dated until I was more certain of the man's place in our lives.

1955 and Beyond: Working with Victims of Poliomyelitis

In 1955, Perón was removed by a coup d'état. He'd held the presidency of Argentina for ten years. I was working ad honorem every morning at the Department of Pediatrics of the Hospital de Clinicas. I had a few private patients, mostly children of friends and relatives whom I was not supposed to charge for my services, according to the cannons of that time. My father continued to support my children and me, despite my medical degree. Later that year, Argentina suffered a severe epidemic of poliomyelitis as the U.S. had the year before. In this emergency, the Institute for Rehabilitation was created to receive patients after their acute phase had been treated at the Hospital for Infectious Diseases. The hospital was known for heroic efforts and for the endless hours of work performed by the few professionals trained to handle respiratory emergencies. The former "Ciudad Infantil" (Children's City), erected by Eva Perón to showcase her dedication to the community, was now empty. It became the site where "The Institute for the Rehabilitation of Disabled" was created and where those polio patients were sent. Pediatricians were to be on call 24 hours, once a week, and when I offered my services, I was hired on the spot. Finally I was earning a salary and could contribute to my family's expenses.

At the new institute, pediatricians, top orthopedic surgeons, and nurses, teamed up to face the challenge of our first experience with poliomyelitis. I marveled at the skill of the six English physical therapists brought in to teach us. I understood the magic of this profession, when in front of the staff, they transformed patients who resembled sacks of bones into children with proper postures. I learned how to deal with a crowd of children and parents whose lives had been abruptly changed in just a few hours by the disease. In shock, I heard parents refuse to bring their handicapped children back home. It was the kind of work that aroused strong emotions in caretakers. No vaccine was available, and I was concerned about bringing the nasty virus home and exposing my two children.

Thankfully, several weeks after the start of the epidemic, the Salk vaccine became available. I was relieved when my children received it. The work at the institute required nights away from home, not welcomed by my family, but I needed a salary so I could continue attending the pediatric wards in the mornings.

Patients needed to stay for long periods of time at the institute to complete rehabilitation, and if allowed out, they had to be accompanied by physicians and nurses. I volunteered to help them - especially over the summer months when my children were visiting their father. Occasionally, my children accompanied me, and during these outings I learned as much as I did from my work in the clinic.

Martha was a 27-year-old secretary when the epidemic struck her. She was completely paralyzed up to her neck and had lost her mother to a heart attack only weeks before Christmas. She asked to go home for the holiday. To fulfill her wish, the chauffeur, a nurse, and I accompanied her in a special van, with heavy hearts, unsure of what to expect. Once we arrived, we rolled the wheelchair toward the front of a very modest house. Suddenly, Martha lifted her head as we crossed the small front garden and said to me, "Doctor, look at this wonderful fig tree!" What a lesson about living that was. Since then, I always try to lift my eyes and find "the fig tree," regardless of how painful a situation might be.

Theresa was another story of resiliency. Like Martha, she could only move her head, but she could breathe on her own. Theresa learned to paint with her mouth and became not only accomplished in the use of the brush, but capable of creating inspired pieces of art. When I moved to Boston, I brought two of them with me.

Memories of two more patients from the institute have remained with me over the years. Debbie and Bianca, both teenagers, had been paralyzed from the waist down. Bianca was an attractive brunette who decided that her life would not stop despite the brutal and sudden limitations imposed on her body. I accompanied them in the patients' van to see a few movies, but with the help of Bianca's mother and a devoted nurse named Anna, we also undertook more ambitious projects. While my children stayed with their father, all five of us went to a small place my father owned near the ocean. My brother volunteered to take four of us in my father's car and Ana went by train. We even managed to take the wheelchairs to the beach and had a great time. We encountered two types of people: those eager to help and others who ignored us.

(Recently in New York City, my daughter Odile and I were walking home from dinner and enjoying a slight breeze. My cell phone rang, the screen displaying that it was an "out of area" call. A woman's voice in Spanish said, "Luisa, this is Bianca." Was I dreaming? The only one by that name I could think of was my patient. I had been thinking about her only two days before, when the swine flu epidemic brought back memories of the epidemic I had lived through so intensely.)

Bianca sent me pictures, and she still looked beautiful. One was taken in Paris with her grandson. Her daughter, a dancer, moved to France, and her parents did too. Bianca even included an old photo from our trip. In it, she, Debbie and I look like three happy youngsters sitting on a stone fence by the sea.

In 1958 I was recruited to work afternoons, six days a week, at the "Center for Respiratory Rehabilitation." The center specialized in the care of patients severely affected by the poliomyelitis epidemic. Their respiratory muscles were paralyzed and they needed mechanical assistance to survive. The large public contribution made it possible to build a model institute run by a man who had been trained in the U.S. by Julius Comroe, a famous pulmonary physiologist. I worked at the center during the day so I wouldn't miss nights at home with my children.

The director was an obsessive disciplinarian. We worked long hours and assembled for our weekly meetings on Saturday afternoons – not a typical schedule in South America. Initially I worked in the instituter's pulmonary lab, where we did arterial punctures to measure blood gases. We inserted a catheter into one of the two main bronchus to measure one lung's volume and then subtracted this number from the total volume of both lungs. That enabled us to determine the ventilation of each lung independently. Many of the tests were performed only on adults. The position of pediatrician opened, and I moved from the lab to clinical work, as I had learned the basics of pulmonary physiology needed in the new position. The institute, known for its strict discipline, was a model in the city, and we received the worst respiratory cases for admissions or for consults as outpatients. I was part of a team treating patients with tetanus, rabies, asthma, and trauma or nervous diseases that affected the respiratory muscles and left patients unable to breathe on their own. Often they were terminal cases. The clinical work was intense and full of drama. One of those dramas hit me. My hairdresser, a young, attractive blond, arrived in a coma as a consequence of a traffic accident, and nothing could be done for her. We treated her with the most advanced available methods, yet these cases opened a Pandora's box of questions heretofore unanswered. Research was part of the institutes's activities allowing me an opportunity to question the methodologies we used.

After several months, it became obvious that I could not continue with the time and study demands of this job and still go to the hospital pediatric ward in the mornings. So I had to quit my morning job.

In addition to caring for acute arrivals, I was responsible for a ward with twenty children permanently living on iron lungs. We noticed that as time went by (months or sometimes years), we had to increase pressure to ventilate them. The iron lung works by creating a negative force around the chest that mimics what the muscles of respiration do normally. That negative force expands the lungs during inspiration. In expiration, the elasticity of the lung causes it to collapse and blow the air out. Why did we need to increase the negative pressure on inspiration? We determined that the lung tissue was losing its elasticity over time. Why? Was it due to the machines that we used, or could it be due to the oxygen we had to add? We did not have the answers. I visited a pathologist to examine the lungs of a child who had died and saw the increase in fibrous tissue that had replaced the elastic fibers. But we did not know the cause. Every day we were confronted with subjects that we needed to learn more about. "Mechanics of Breathing" was a new field for me and it involved physics and mathematics. I jumped into it.

I also did research measuring our observations on breathing that I incorporated in my doctoral thesis. I longed for a chance to visit one of the centers in the U.S. that generated much of the pivotal information on the subject. During the polio epidemic, the director (Dr. Aquiles Roncoroni), received help from two consultants from Boston. Dr. James Whittenberger and Dr. Benjamin Ferris arrived from the Harvard School of Public Health and so impressed our director, that he suggested I visit their department in Boston. His suggestion impacted the rest of my life.

Visiting the North Shore in 1962 during a first trip to Boston

The usual way for a young scientist to travel abroad was to earn a fellowship provided by an institution. Typically, a yearlong absence was involved. I, divorced and with two children, couldn't make so extended a trip. I was, however, able to go for the three months that my children stayed with their father. My father, with his usual generosity, financed my trip. As best as I could, I used available resources to reduce the costs.

Later, as the only pediatrician in the institute, I became one of only two pediatricians invited for membership in the prestigious National Council for Research. The other pediatrician, Dr. Giannantonio, was internationally known for having described the uremic-hemolytic syndrome.

I arrived in Boston on January 7, 1962, during a bitter winter. I remember that day vividly and recall coming from the airport through the Callahan Tunnel under the ocean and the marvel of it. I had never seen snow. Everything was covered with it, and it was not until the last days of my stay, with a bit warmer weather, that I could see green patches on the ground.

I resided at the YWCA in Copley Square. There was no tall John Hancock building then to obscure the view of the square from my window. At breakfast the first day, I met a lovely, elderly woman with whom I remained friends. Her husband ran an ashram for a peace organization. Following her mistaken advice, for two days, I rode the "T" in the wrong direction - all the way to Cambridge - to go to the School of Public Health, which was in the opposite direction on Huntington Avenue.

I worked in the Physiology Department under the direction of the peerless Dr. Jere Mead. The informal climate that I encountered in academia at Harvard was new to me, and I liked it instantly. The desk to which I was assigned was in the office of Bob Frank, an assistant professor who was attractive, single, and charming. With my limited English, useful mainly to read the most difficult scientific papers, I tried to understand what my colleagues were saying.

Dr. Benjamin Ferris, who had been the consultant in Argentina, was my official sponsor. One weekend he invited me to his elegant family home in Weston. Another weekend after a heavy snowstorm had kept me inside, Dr. William Forbes invited me to his home in Milton "to see the snow in the country." There I met his wife, also a distinguished physician. The department's secretaries found the time on another weekend to take me to the North Shore and show me the snow on the rocks in Rockport. I managed those visits wearing the thick nutria coat I had brought with me. In a mere three months, and with an introduction given to me by a friend in Argentina, I met wonderful people both socially and at work. I enjoyed the magic of a first concert at Symphony Hall. When I went shopping in Boston, the sales ladies noticed my accent. "Are you a student?" they asked. One urged me to see the Van Gogh exhibit at the Museum of Fine Arts (MFA), which I did and I loved, being a devotee of European art. I made repeated visits to the MFA. Bostonians were proud of their city, and I was learning to love it too.

At Harvard, my supervisor, Jere Mead, was not only a brilliant researcher, but a fair and gentle man. To my surprise, I discovered that Dr. Mead had designed the instruments used in his research. I'd gone to the United States thinking that engineers had designed the research equipment physicians used. Sophisticated equipment was actually designed based on suggestions from the researchers themselves. The experiments, no matter how uncomfortable, were performed on the researchers themselves – for example, a catheter would be put through the nose and into the subject's stomach. I participated in these experiments too.

During my brief tenure, I also met Dr. Clement Smith, a specialist in newborns. One of the main challenges of newborns has to do with the initiation of respiration. In the womb, the lungs are full of liquid and the transition to air is essential, but often difficult, and may require the use of assisted respiration.

I noticed that Dr. Smith had been given only one room at Children's Hospital. Yet in that small room today's neonatology services and the field of neonatology itself was born.

As my visit came to its close, I prepared to return to Argentina. I marveled at the independence American women seemed to have. But I also noted what a striking minority they were in the freshman class of the Harvard Medical School. I had discovered a new world, one I had to leave and feared I might never see again.

I cried all the way on my bus ride from Boston to New York, where I would catch my plane home. Sitting next to me was a black woman from the Dominican Republic who, despite the prejudice against black persons, was happy to be in America. I went to the Metropolitan Museum of Art and said good-bye to the Rodin sculptures, especially one of my favorites, "The Hand of God." Given the poor economic potential of my academic career in Argentina, I did not foresee the likelihood of having enough money to make another visit to Boston. I felt, sadly, that I was returning to remain in Argentina forever.

Nevertheless, during the next few years, I plotted an eventual emigration to America. Friends of mine also sought better futures in the United States. Felix had already emigrated with his family. He found a three-year Ph.D. course in Miami to which I could apply. I sent my CV and could have been accepted, but when I informed my enlightened Georgina of my plans, she opposed the move on the grounds that she would not attend Miami's segregated schools. Finally, three years after my initial visit, I wrote a letter to Jere Mead asking if I could somehow return to the Department of Physiology. I can only speculate that my dedication as a fellow during my brief visit suggested to him that I had potential to be trained further. He gave me a position that included an immigrant visa for me, as well as my children.

In 1965, I departed for North America with Georgina, now 15, and Marcelo, 13. Leaving Argentina was not easy. I had family and friends I had to part with, and of course there was my father - my biggest support and best friend. Although he had remarried in 1952 and was very happy, it was hard to leave him. At the airport when I left, among the crowd were four children on assisted ventilation whom I had treated and who had come to say goodbye.

4

Arrival in North America, 1965-1973

I arrived in Boston in 1965. My decision to come was perhaps the most significant of my professional life. I was left behind so many of the things that I valued: my career, my friends, and mostly, the protection of my father. The separation from him was especially cruel. What initially made it bearable was his promise to visit for long periods – but he never did.

This arrival, as opposed to my first landing in 1962, was an altogether different experience. I came with my two children, two suitcases and the silverware in my handbag. As the plane touched down, my children began complaining and bickering, as children do. I realized that, like Hernando Cortes, I had "to burn my ships." I gave each child a gentle slap on the cheek and ordered them to be still. I was here to build a home for them and a career for me, and they had to cooperate. But settling down was no small task. Georgina was somewhat depressed, and Marcelo was suffering from what may have been ADD, an unknown diagnosis at that time.

We initially spent a few days at the home of Janet and Jeff – friends I had met during my previous visit. I rented an apartment in Brookline only a few blocks from the highly rated high school Georgina would attend. Around the corner was Marcelo's elementary school. Their education did not proceed as smoothly as I had hoped. We all paid a price for their having been pulled out of their familiar milieu. Georgina had bouts of depression, and Marcelo was relegated to a second-class citizen's status by his teacher who had apparently decided that foreigners were not worth her efforts.

Before the move, I had never done my own house cleaning or cooking. Now I had to cope with the reality of those daily chores. At the same time, I was propelled into a fascinating work situation but one for which I had not been fully trained. It was a hard first year. I used to call my father and cry because I missed him, but I knew I could not unload my frustrations on him.

Professionally, my appointment at Harvard turned out to be the biggest challenge. During my previous stint in Boston, I'd been a Fellow in the Department of Physiology. Now I was a research associate in that department. I worked closely with Jere Mead and his team – his title was Professor of Physiology at the School of Public Health. Dr. Mead was not only a giant in terms of his thoughts and original research, but in terms of his teaching ability as well. Dr. Mead explained the most complex ideas in clear and simple terms. He transformed formidable problems into manageable ones. His fairness to others was also touching.

Originally Dr. Mead had in mind that I would work with Dr. Mary Ellen Wohl to develop techniques in pulmonary pediatrics. The project took take place at Children's Hospital under the auspices of the Harvard School of Public Health. Only recently, in 2009, did I read a lengthy and impressive obituary of Dr. Wohl in the *Boston Globe* which described her distinguished career. My experience working with her, however, was not among my happiest memories. I had trouble understanding her colloquial English, and as colleagues, we were not compatible. We did one project together, the results of which were published, but I felt miserable as I worked merely as a technician. One of my most vivid memories of that time is of being reprimanded by her and the hospital for walking in a corridor without a white coat. I was dressed only in the blue surgical set of pants and blouse that people now wear even in the street.

It was suggested that I work on two other projects at the Department of Physiology. One pertained to the mathematical curve that describes the flow of air through the larynx; the other described the forces that determine the existence of a pleural exudate. Pleural effusion refers to the excess fluid that accumulates between the two pleural layers, the virtual fluid-filled space that surrounds the lungs. Excessive amounts of such fluid can impair breathing by limiting the expansion of the lungs during ventilation. They were ambitious projects even for the very skilled, but in terms of a proper background, I wasn't well matched to the tasks. My training was mainly clinical; I had little manual ability, and I lacked a basic understanding and an intuitive sense of the equipment that we had to use. I was at a huge disadvantage as those devices were integral to comprehending what we'd observed.

I tried my best. Even in Argentina, after I'd finished medical school, I studied calculus with a private tutor to increase my knowledge of math. In Boston, too, I attended math classes at Harvard. Some of the physics required a deeper level of math than I possessed. I could study and understand these subjects, but I could not add ideas to advance the subject. I published an article about the voluntary control of the diaphragm, an important respiratory muscle, based on work I had done in Argentina, but no original paper came out of those years.

I felt frustrated. Dr. Mead referred to me as a pediatrician when introducing me to visitors, but he never made me believe I was worthless for failing to reach his level. Still, I felt that I was failing at the work, a failure I dream about even to this day.

About five years after my arrival, I worked under the auspices of the Department of Pathology at Children's Hospital. The project consisted of inflating lungs at postmortem and studying and measuring histological images of those specimens. I was much more comfortable dealing with histological images than I'd been trying to understand the equipment I had to deal with at the School of Public Health.

At the same time that I was learning about the lung, I was immersed in Pediatric Pathology, working with a renowned teacher Gordon Vawter, the principal collaborator of Sidney Farber - the Pathologist-in-Chief. Pathology was closer to my clinical training than the Mechanics of Breathing. It was "sink or swim" due to the solitary manner in which I had to do my research. Even as I struggled, the primitive methods of research I used were becoming obsolete, replaced by computerized technologies.

For these reasons and to support my family, I made the decision to leave the Department of Pathology at Children's Hospital and to return to Pediatrics, the field for which I had originally been trained. I had already been moonlighting as a pediatrician at Dedham Medical Associates (DMA) to help pay for Marcelo's private school. When one of their pediatricians left giving only short notice, I began to work there full-time.

Still, I dreamed that one day I could afford to go back to be near Dr. Vawter, the master who taught me so much about pediatric pathology.

Unfortunately he died, but his teachings and the conferences I had attended at Children's Hospital enhanced my knowledge of medicine in ways I still value. When I left Children's Hospital, I knew that I was leaving a tremendous learning opportunity, but I was also grateful for my time there. As much as I admired research, I became aware that my calling was to clinical pediatrics.

And so life began anew in 1973 at DMA. As a moonlighter, I'd already had some experience in a private pediatrics practice – at least as practiced by Dr. David Winter. With the backup of Children's Hospital, I enjoyed my full-time work at DMA, a pleasure that sustained me through almost every day.

During this period my personal life was changing even more dramatically. In Argentina, before our return to the States, I'd met a man through two friends from Boston. I recall the day I received a fateful call from the visitor to Argentina.

"Hello, I'm Florian Weissenborn from Boston - a friend of Janet and Jeff. They asked me to see you," said the stranger. "They sent you a small gift."

Imagining that a foreigner might want to see the countryside, I politely promised him a visit to my father's quinta, saying that I looked forward to meeting him. Poor weather and family complications required that we reschedule, and we agreed instead to have coffee at the beautiful Richmond café instead.

Upon meeting, the man looked so young, for a moment I thought I should introduce him to my daughter Georgina. He wore a raincoat and his beret gave him a European look. He had a strong English accent and fine manners. Politely, we shook hands and he introduced himself again, saying he'd be in Argentina for the week - visiting relatives who had emigrated from Germany during the Nazi years.

Our conversation was distant yet cordial. Although he lived in Boston, Florian mentioned that he had spent some time in Argentina. I shared my enthusiasm for Boston and the critical fact that I had two children and that any change would only be possible if they were included.. I felt that this last piece of information moved him. When he left Argentina, I wasn't sure if I would see him again. However, a few months later, Florian sent me a friendly letter. I answered it properly, assuming that this handsome man and the titillating world I'd discovered in Boston were forever lost to me.

When, to my surprise, I was offered the position at The Harvard School of Public Health, not only was I able to return to Boston, but as fate would have it, I resumed my friendship with Florian as well.

When I stayed with Janet and Jeff, since Florian was a frequent visitor to their home, we met again. Once again I found his company pleasant.

Resettling my family in the midst of a bitter winter was no small task ,and my friends mobilized to help us. Janet borrowed two mattresses from her sister and an old chair (that I refurbished and still treasure). Florian accompanied me to purchase furniture and other housewares - errands that allowed me to appreciate his good taste. He also helped with my driving. I had obtained an international license in Buenos Aires before my departure, but I lacked driving experience. Florian was a patient copilot and gave sound guidance (as did Marcelo, at 13, whom my father had already taught how to drive). After a few weeks, I learned from friends that Florian was on a ski trip, and for the first time I realized I missed his company.

When he returned, Florian called again. How my life brightened with invitations to an art auction, a party at Florian's friends, a lecture by Felix Green – or a gourmet dinner at Florian's home. There I met a group of his politically-minded acquaintances. (Florian and my children and I marched to protest the War in Vietnam.) I knew little about Florian's personal life, but quickly discovered his vast knowledge - of literature, history and the world. He brought interesting conversation into my home and shared himself with my children – even at the risk of enduring my cooking. (Fortunately, Georgina took up cooking, delighting us with her new skill.) Soon, Florian became a frequent visitor, competing with a few other men who showed an interest in me. A divorcée had more of a chance to remarry in the States than in Argentina. I was aware of this and hoped to marry again someday.

Quite suddenly, Florian left for Europe. I believed he'd done so to create some distance between us. But his trip did not last long. A severe and persistent toothache brought him back in poor shape. He welcomed my support, and we bonded even more strongly. Should I have been alarmed by his degree of emotional collapse due to a toothache? Perhaps? If it was a warning, I ignored it. Had I not, I would have seen it as a dependency that would last many years. From his point of view, I was a physician who held the secrets that he, a hypochondriac, craved. He had also been love-deprived and felt nurtured by me.

My difficult first year in America – coping with work and resettlement - ended on a celebratory note. I gave a surprise birthday party for Florian on December 31st, 1965. Not long afterward, I met Hilde and Walter, Boston-based relatives of Florian's stepfather and the only family contact Florian made in the States.

"Why don't you get married?" Hilde asked me one day.

"We cannot afford a change of housing now," I said.

"Florian's parents are rich," she said.

That was news to me. The possibility of receiving help from his parents had a magnetic effect on me, and I saw marrying him as a real possibility.

A few months later, I saw an ad for a house in Nahant. The previous summer, Florian had driven me to the beaches of this lovely and isolated island and my lifelong yearning for a house by the sea grew. The two of us went to see it, and on the way back to my home, we discussed the magic issue - marriage. We already had plans to travel around New England for few days; the sites he chose to visit revealed his utterly sophisticated taste and enchanted me. His knowledge of liquors was part of his gentleman's culture. I learned that Port wine can be drunk as an aperitif before dinner in addition to serving it with dessert. At about this time his mother came to visit and meet me. Helping her unpack, I saw a bottle of scotch in her suitcase. It was the first time I'd seen an elegant lady carrying such a thing. I didn't give it much thought at the time. My father's habit of drinking wine mixed with soda had not prepared me for the more sophisticated world in which I now lived. Nor did it prepare me for the dangerous one I was about to enter permanently.

Even during our courtship, I knew little of Florian's background. He rarely spoke of his parents or childhood. He was born in Leipzig, Germany, on December 31, 1931. It was the same year that Hitler began his official career. Florian's mother, Edith, belonged to a well-to-do Jewish family. Hellmuth, Florian's father, was born into a Lutheran family of artists, musicians and painters. His Jewish maternal grandfather did not agree with his daughter's choice of husbands, and after the wedding did not allow his daughter and her baby to enter his home. Only the maternal grandmother met them and only in public places. Young Hellmuth and his father Fritz were professors at the Academy of Arts. The Gestapo became aware of Hellmuth's opposition to Hitler's ideas through a maid and summoned him to their headquarters for an investigation. Hellmuth and his father had already been dismissed from positions at the Academy, but now Hellmuth found his situation even more compromised because he had married a Jew. For that reason, on one of his regular sailing trips with his painter friends, he decided not to sail back to Germany. That left Florian alone with his mother – both of them abandoned by the father.

Due to the rise of Nazi Germany, the maternal grandparents had a change of heart about their daughter and her child, and they decided to leave Germany and to bring them along. They left early enough to be able to take a few possessions, but of course they left behind their homes, other family members, and friends. Under these difficult circumstances, Florian, at six, was sent to Italy to the first school created by Maria Montessori. He stayed there by himself for six months until an aunt took him to London where Florian was reunited with his mother. It was not an idyllic reunion, though, with the Nazis bombing London steadily. Even late in his life, the noise of broken glass deeply disturbed Florian.

During Florian's family exodus from Europe, the adults had to cross the Pyrenees to reach England. His maternal grandfather died in this effort. With London besieged after the family's arrival, Florian was sent to Yorkshire where his mother chose a good Christian school – perhaps to keep him safe. He was to continue his education there. But in Yorkshire, Florian was both a foreigner and a Jew which must have increased his feelings of isolation. He would remember the obligatory, daily visits to church and the severe punishments received with a stick for minor faults.

Meanwhile, Florian's father, a citizen of an enemy country, had been interned near London for two years. Florian's parents were able to meet again, and they divorced. Hellmuth stayed in London, where he remarried and continued his career as a painter. For reasons I do not know, Hellmuth had Florian baptized even though Hellmuth was not a religious Christian himself.

Florian's mother, the youngest of three sisters, had lived a pampered life before her marriage. Unprepared for the difficult circumstances the war brought on, she needed assistance to bring up Florian. The best she could do was to stay near his school in Yorkshire. In 1943, she obtained a United States visa and managed to obtain a cabin on a ship to cross the Atlantic with her child. Florian was 12. He and his mother traveled in a convoy to protect ships from the German submarines and their torpedoes. Since it had taken months to find a ship, by the time they arrived in New York, their visa had expired. Florian and his mother stayed at Ellis Island a long time until a woman who was serving their meals offered to contact

Edith's New York uncle, Max, who signed an affidavit which allowed Florian and his mother into the U.S.

Max was a successful fur merchant for whom Florian's grandfather had worked and who had an agency in London. Once in New York, Florian lived with his mother and grandmother in a hotel until his mother left for Argentina to marry the brother of her brother-in-law. Florian remained in New York with his maternal grandmother. He was 14 at the time.

Upon his grandmother's death, Florian went to Argentina where he attended an English boarding school, spending weekends with his German-speaking mother and stepfather. Florian had never learned Spanish well. Florian's stepfather owned a sweater factory. For that reason, instead of sending Florian to college, his mother sent him to a study at a technical institute in Lowell, Massachusetts. Florian didn't feel that going to a technical institute suited his interests, but he obeyed and went. (He later completed a master's degree program in journalism at Boston University, a better fit for his skills and inclinations.)

When he was 17, Florian visited his father in London. Hellmuth was a formidable man, an egotist like many artists, who could be arrogant and domineering though at other times he was tender and very generous. Young Florian was too sensitive to establish a close relationship with him. Later, when we were married. As a couple we became closer to Hellmuth and enjoyed his company, ignoring his sharp criticisms and those of his similarly critical second wife. Florian rarely spoke about his difficult past, but during the course of the thirty years of our relationship, bits and pieces emerged that helped me try to put together the puzzle that was my husband.

Back in Boston, in 1966, events led quickly to our plan to marriage. Florian's mother was told, and she approved of our wedding. We looked for housing and found an old, inexpensive yet elegant apartment for rent with the help of an experienced real estate agent determined to help with my plans. The apartment had five bedrooms, a small, covered sunny patio, a bar, and a wide entrance hall with black and white linoleum squares. We could not ask for more. We had planned to have our wedding at the ceremonial room of the Harvard Divinity School, but when we arrived, we found it under repair. We ended up at the apartment of the Unitarian Universalist Fellow candidate who married us. God did not participate in our brief ceremony, which was followed by a lunch with few friends.

During our courtship, Florian managed to relate well to both my children. Georgina was a true intellectual from very early in her life. She and Florian had deep conversations covering a variety of subjects including politics. With Marcelo, Florian shared themes of interest to boys, like cars. In later years, Florian lamented that he could not forge a deeper relationship with Marcelo, and yet Marcelo still has warm feelings for his stepfather. Yet these harmonic beginnings did not stop either Georgina or Marcelo from provoking us. My life became difficult trying to please everybody while attending to the challenging demands of my work.

In 1969, Florian's father invited us to go to Europe. I returned pregnant from that trip. Our Odile Antoinette was born in December of 1969. Georgina, at 20 years old and angered at my pregnancy, decided to return to Argentina and lost her green card. She dropped out of Sarah Lawrence College in the United States and went to work for her paternal grandfather, Dr. Gregorio Bermann, as a secretary, in Cordoba, Argentina. Dr. Bermann was a prestigious psychiatrist, well known for his leftist ideas. Georgina's communications with me grew sparse during that period.

My son Marcelo, after completing four years in a private high school, moved away from home. It was the sixties and he shared in the culture of the times. He experimented with drugs. How much this influenced his future, I cannot know.

While still working at the Harvard School of Public Health, I passed three required courses and in 1969, pregnant with my daughter Odile, the three-day exam from the Massachusetts Board of Medicine. In order to stop foreign visiting doctors from remaining in Boston, the Board of Medicine had added the college courses to make the board exam in Massachusetts particularly difficult. (Twenty years before those exams, and pregnant with Georgina, I'd passed the exam corresponding to the third year of medical school when I was in Argentina.)

Florian's career as the editor of a weekly textile publication ended a few years into our marriage when he was laid off. While it's true Florian often called in sick, the final putsch occurred when he chose a black model for use in a story, which displeased the owners and their Southern readers. Work was never going to be Florian's strength. Except for a job working for a Catholic Community College, he never found a job that satisfied him.

Florian went through long periods of searching for employment, suffering from the depression that accompanies such frustrating efforts. Given Florian's difficulties, and after Odile's birth, I accepted that I had to be the main wage earner. His cousin, an academic mathematician, confronted me with that reality on one of his rare visits. The impact must have been significant because I still vividly recall our discussion, during the few moments that Florian was absent from our living room. His cousin pointed out that we needed more than what Children's Hospital offered me as a salary. The discussion was a factor in my decision to accept working full time as a pediatrician in Dedham. I would give up, at least for the time, my academic medical career. This financial solution would bring about another type of crisis: I had to be available to work at night.

My new job at DMA involved 24-hour service—grueling in bad weather with my long night commute. I needed to be near my office during my days and nights on call. I looked for a room to rent in the area. Of course, given Florian's moods, our personal relationship was already imperfect at best. I became aware than in a family dynamic as tense as ours, brief separations only led to more conflict, and I had been a divorced mother for many years. I decided on the alternative that was to move *en famille*, a choice that was hard for my husband-unless he chose the site. I found a medium size house for rent, ideal given our precarious financial situation, but Florian rejected it.

A few days after rejecting it, and just before Florian would lose his job, he called and asked me to look at a house he found for sale at 150 Court Street in Dedham. It was an enchanting palace with decorated glass panels in the windows, crystal lead cases in the dining room and a copper bell covering the top of the fireplace in the living room. There was a large garden, five bedrooms, a basement, and a third floor. I drove back to our apartment wondering how we could possibly afford such a house. First, we needed enough for a down payment.

I remembered that I had an unused pension fund from my years at the Harvard School of Public Health. It could be withdrawn as cash. But, we needed double its value. Gifts from Florian's family provided the other half, and we obtained a mortgage. Still, we needed an extra five hundred dollars to hold the land next to the house for a year. The following year, my father sold his apartment in Argentina. Half of the sale money went to my brother, half to me. Florian's family again contributed half of the cost, enabling us to add the extra land to our garden and to pay in cash. By then Florian had been laid off, a casualty of the college's personnel changes. Paying the mortgage seemed a huge responsibility for me. As the years went by, my position as a community doctor was consolidated and the burden seemed lighter. The beautiful house that I viewed as an imposition when I first moved in became a source of comfort.

Aside from playing squash or tennis, Florian became less and less interested in social activities, outings or travel. The wife of one of his playmates explained to me that we were "squash widows" since the men left their energy on the courts. Florian had been brought up without much touching or tender gestures and could not initiate physical contact. Odile recalls we did not go out as a family. He would take her to the ballet or the theater on weekends while I was on call and he was the parent in charge. When I took her out on weekends, he didn't join us. We gave up our Symphony seats and went out only occasionally. If I organized a dinner party, he complained. Even so I persisted in hosting these events.

Looking back, I understand the role alcohol was playing in our lives. but at the time I was unaware of it. Many problems, whatever their apparent cause, stemmed from Florian's alcoholism. For one thing, he couldn't sleep. I ended up sleeping in the guest room to cope with the demands of work the next day. He became master of our bedroom in spite of the fact that my clothes were there; often I couldn't use my vanity. Because of his insomnia, he needed silence during the day. He could only tolerate a low tone of voice, which was hard for me given the stress of my daily life, his inconsistent behavior, and my Latino-Jewish background. He frequently missed work when he did have a job and when he did, I was the one who had to call and make excuses. Without knowing I was doing so, I played the role of the perfect codependent and enabler.

Our interactions were typical for a couple when one of the partners is an alcoholic, but I did not know that then. I had to plan how to say things to him so he would not react with the kind of offensive answer that I found hard to accept. I later learned the expression "walking on eggshells." Not only did the ring of the phone bother him, but also any conversation I had to carry on.

"Why do you need to talk for so long?" he'd whine.

He found any intrusion from the outside intolerable, including house guests. He wanted my sole attention and yet used no nice words – no sweeteners – to obtain it. It was my duty to take care of him and the house and to do it perfectly. Of course my supporting us didn't enter into the equation.

He helped with house chores, but I never knew when to count on him. 'When' depended on his state of sobriety and his level of depression.

In terms of money, we struggled. Florian's mother helped with the down payment of the house in Dedham and sent me monthly money for a live-in maid, but I used this to pay in part for Odile's private elementary school. When Odile reached high school and college, Florian's aunt Lilly paid for it.

Our love of Odile, was the relationship's only glue. Odile broke down Florian's defensive barriers – the walls he'd built to resist loving and the hurt loving can bring. When Odile was a small child, he treated her with tenderness but closed up like a porcupine in his later years when he could not tolerate the pain his drinking caused her. He had been brought up under strict discipline, and even though he resented it, he could not accept the more lax child-rearing standards predominant at the time and that I endorsed. That was also a source of conflict that our child may have sensed.

Florian was a serious reader with a fine critical mind, and he was well informed when it came to history and politics. He often reached bitter philosophical conclusions, but I felt he had a noble core. Unfortunately, alcohol created the self-depreciation hat best characterized him and erased much of the good that might have come from his fine mind. Drinking twisted his thoughts and warped his comments so that he was constantly destructive. I encouraged him to look at our home as a temple, one that could isolate us from the rest of a world that he found troubling. I urged him to be thankful for all that we had. He could not be.

I tried the help of psychologists and psychiatrists: none of them guessed his problem. It took our daughter, concerned about Florian, to bring up his drinking. Knowledge about alcoholism, the Twelve Step programs and Al Anon were not as widespread as they are today. Unbeknown to me, Florian was an alcoholic, and that reality eventually ended our marriage and finally - his life. Did it affect me so much that in time I was diagnosed with cancer? I am a doctor, but I cannot answer that question.

5

Pediatrics in Dedham, 1973-2005

Dedham is a historic town southwest of Boston, a half hour drive from downtown. Dedham Medical Associates (DMA) was established in 1937 as an independent multi-specialty group of physicians and dentists.

As mentioned earlier, when I initially begin moonlighting there, I didn't have my own office, so when they closed at 5 pm, I was on-call - which meant staying nearby in case a patient needed care. I waited at the public library, and occasionally, I'd return to the empty offices, see a child, and only then received compensation.

When the income for the Children's Hospital research project that paid my salary waned, I added day-work hours at DMA. Then also, I was paid on a fee-for-service basis: no patients seen, no income. Later, when DMA routinely used after-hours moonlighters they paid on an hourly basis, regardless of how many patients were seen.

As I've written, Dr. William Winter, the pediatrician I worked with most closely, was a brilliant diagnostician. In 1973, the second pediatrician in the group left on short notice. By then I had become acquainted with the group's high standards. At the same time, I saw no future for me at Children's Hospital and also recognized I was better at clinical work than research. I asked Dr. Winter if I could fill the prospective vacant position. My best credential was the work I had already done. I would be the only foreign graduate, the only woman and perhaps the only Jew in the group, but he gave me the job on the spot. As one of the regular physicians, my duties suddenly increased. I was on-call every other night and on weekends.

The offices of DMA occupied a Cape Cod styled chalet, which was once a private residence in an exclusive area on High Street. The back of our "office building" overlooked a branch of the Charles River.

I felt as if I had arrived at a safe harbor when patients and other members of the group accepted me. To protect me and keep me company when I worked alone at night, I took Daphne with me - a shepherd I loved and had acquired from a shelter.

The opportunity to provide state-of-the-art care in association with Children's Hospital was exhilarating. The patients got used to my non-native accent and in some cases their mothers corrected my English. Once when I gave a mother instructions to "Put one drop in every ear," she told me gently, "One drop in each ear." Another mother, upon seeing a female doctor in the practice for the first time, commented, "It was worth paying for the visit just so my son can see that women can be doctors and not only nurses."

As the first woman doctor in my group, I made a point of being feminine in my appearance and efficient in my work – initiating a standard that quickly characterized our practice. When I retired, there were more women pediatricians than men at DMA - reflecting a national trend. During my years at DMA, I received the same pay as my male colleagues, an accommodation that many women still struggle to obtain.

Six months after I started working full-time, another established pediatrician joined our group. We were three partners, which meant fewer days on call but a bigger case load as my own practice grew. Until I joined DMA, I had worked mainly in academic settings. Now and with the help of Dr. Winter, I was busy learning more of the banal, hands-on aspects of practical pediatrics.

The strong link between DMA and leading area hospitals, including Boston Children's Hospital, reassured me that my career and the high medical standards I valued would continue even though I no longer worked for the hospital. Patients drove many miles to come to DMA and we were committed to fulfilling their expectations by providing the best possible care. I enjoyed the challenge, and I wanted to continually be updated on the advances in medicine. I attended weekly conferences and whole-day seminars at the Children's Hospital and regularly read the pediatric journals.

Pediatrics is best practiced as a team. Professionals and auxiliary personnel need to share expertise and relate to the individual personalities of the young patients. Comparing how pediatrics was practiced then to now, I worry that the overuse of computers might threaten the direct relationship of the pediatric team to their patients – but time will tell.

When I started working at DMA, I shared my secretary, Arlene, with other doctors. But as my practice grew, I was allowed to have my own secretary. My secretaries represented me to my patients, and they knew how to organize my work. They grew skillful in assessing the degree of urgency of a parent's concern. They reassured the parents and provided proper answers to many of their questions. I have fond memories of some of my secretaries, and I developed a strong emotional tie to some of them. They helped when a patient first called, and they helped to ease patients while they waited for me. They handled communications with pharmacies and insurance companies. We shared concerns about the patients who were at risk because of either the severity of their illness or when family or social situations complicated their illness. We made joint efforts not to miss a patient's call. In my absence, my secretary helped provide the continuity of my care.

Often, I became the pediatrician of my own secretary's children. Then we functioned as a team in both roles – the effort often resulting in a lifelong bond. An example that occurred in later years was my dear friend and former secretary, Margie. Margie was devoted to me and to my patients. In later years we stayed in touch. She sent me cards and updated me as her children grew up and let me know when she first became a grandmother. Years later, one of her daughters helped me refurbish the bathrooms in my new apartment. She refused to charge because, in her words, "You took good care of my family."

At times I placed heavy demands on my staff. That inspired devotion from some and annoyance from others. DMA resolved these workload issues by assigning me one secretary and one nurse, thus allowing me to create a team. We were committed to optimal care. We failed at times as humans do, but our goal inspired us during hours of hard work. The nurse would bring the patient in and, in a relaxed manner, ask the reason for the visit, gathering information from a few essential questions. The nurse's personal touches created an atmosphere of caring that facilitated my own work. Each nurse had her own style (there were no male nurses then). Diane never failed to smile; Joanne, equally efficient, was more severe. It was important that we kept up with our daily schedule, and when we fell behind, we tried not to make the patient responsible with comments like, "We're very busy today" - a couched request to shorten their visit which is not what a patient wants to hear from their doctor.

When I entered the examination room, my patient would already have changed into a gown, which allowed for an easier and more thorough exam. Examining a child who is fully undressed was important, and I could be on the lookout for issues besides those that prompted their appointment. In today's busy pediatric examination rooms, children are often seen fully clothed, and the exam is usually limited to the organ related to the complaint that initiated the appointment.

The young patients had their own agendas. Often an appointment might begin with the child giving me a work of art – a detailed drawing of my office. A typical drawing might include the young artist as a patient, lying on the examining table and attached to imaginary equipment with me standing beside the patient – my rings showing on my fingers. Children were good critics of my personal appearance. They were fascinated by details like shoes or jewelry. On one occasion I allowed a toddler to wear my necklace to obtain her cooperation. That became part of our routine. Once, as I bent over to listen to the heart of a two-year-old blond boy, he raised his head, looked at me with his large, brown eyes and said, "smell," acknowledging my French perfume. Occasionally I heard disapproving comments like, "The color of your hair is different today."

When I first began to work at DMA in the early seventies, our office was open from nine to five. I wanted to stay open beyond noon on Saturdays and needed to submit a written request to the board of directors. I had noticed that children were out of school and their bicycle accidents and ear aches did not accommodate our restricted schedule. Instead of commuting to tend to every patient needing care, I was allowed to remain alone in the building for a few more hours. A wooden-board with an attached wrapping, imitating a baby-bunting, was my only helper when I needed to restrain a little one who needed stitches. On some weekends or late nights I brought my German Shepard along in hopes that she would provide some security.

In the late seventies, we moved to offices in a larger edifice that overlooked a branch of the Charles River and that was built to our own specifications. From its windows, my patients and I were able to gaze at the birds and the ever-changing vegetation of a New England marsh.

In the eighties, "after-hours" became routine for pediatricians in the Boston area, and our office followed the trend. After 5 p.m., helped by another team of health workers, we stayed on. In the nineties, the younger doctors refused the extended long hours, and once again, DMA began hiring doctors who moonlighted. When the office was closed, we answered night calls from our homes. I found it hard, after sleepless nights, to endure an entire new day of work. Eventually, I had to hire a lawyer to be permitted to have a few hours of sleep and let our nurse practitioner fill in for me. Once more, things changed in a direction I had pioneered. Soon after my effort, nurses started answering night calls in most pediatric offices. Doctors were called only when consultations were necessary.

As the way medicine was practiced began to change, it became harder to build and to count on support from an ideal team. In the late nineties, nurse assistants, trained only on the basics, brought patients to the examining room. I missed the more experienced nurses who had previously performed this job and who also kept track of the pace of my work while contributing to a smooth work flow.

To avoid crowding and long wait times, my secretary kept a list of patients who would need more of my time and she allocated double slots of time for them. The computer showed gaps in my daily schedule for "coffee breaks" and for lunches that were actually times left open for emergencies or to accommodate a heavier than usual patient load. When the time I needed for a patient visit wasn't enough, I made myself available for an added "after hour" visit. In this way, I circumvented the constraints often imposed by insurance companies - avid to see more income produced during a particular time period, and not paying for the "after hour" visits that are needed in more complicated cases.

A pool of secretaries who recognize a patient only by their Social Security or record number is, sadly, today's norm. It is a shame, because when the people at the reception desk are familiar with a patient, it eases the natural tension of visiting the doctor. Computers, not patients, are center stage now in the reception area. They were initially used in my office for administrative purposes only. Patients' records were typed or recorded by hand. Paper notes allowed us to write in special remarks which were useful when seeing a patient with whom one was not familiar. Today, the information included in the medical record is constricted by the software.

The computer now sits at the doctor's desk in the examining room and limits the time of direct visual contact with the patient. Inspection, taking time to look at the patient, used to be the first step of diagnosis; observation was emphasized. Today instead of facing the patient as we used to do, the Harvard Medical students are taken to a museum to learn to observe.

The scene in a pediatrics office is very different from the flashy emergency room action seen on television. We take care of the children from birth to college graduation. A large part of our task is preventive medicine. We have an opportunity to provide counsel and education to the child and the family on crucial aspects of their lives. We take pride in the accomplishments of our patients, and we experience pain with their failings. We also plan an important role in the prevention of acute and chronic diseases. Our daily world is so rich in human experiences that we often feel the need to share it with others. This is perhaps why many doctors, myself included, like to write about their work.

My personal life was interwoven with the new professional developments. I was dealing with a difficult marriage, a young child at home and two older children in faraway places. I was also trying to help my beloved and aging father. In this chapter I chose my professional life, but of course my personal life and my professional life were never entirely separate. One affected the other as more and more professional women understand today.

Like most working mothers, I needed to start the day organizing my home. I liked to leave for work with at least the beds made. It gave me the feeling, sometimes illusory, that my private life was in order. Before Odile reached school age, I needed the help of a nanny. When Odile started school, I had to find after-school help. Florian would look after her at times but the final responsibility for her care was mine. I could never teach my children to cooperate and move quickly in the mornings. If I was stressed and in a hurry, my mood wasn't always gentle.

Reading the *New York Times* with my cup of tea, allowing myself a few minutes to think about my world and the larger one we live in, was a luxury I had to postpone until a day came when I'd have no children at home. I had to arrive later than the other pediatrician to take care of my child. When she grew up, I continued to enjoy the privilege of arriving late, never knowing when I would be finished in the evening.

When I arrived late at the office, I had to find a parking place amid snow banks and rain puddles. When finally I reached my desk, several small pink notes with patients' messages were sitting on a large crystal square marked "IN." Messages had already been screened by my secretary who handled the urgent ones. But I was mindful that behind each pink note a parent waited with varying degrees of anxiety. There was also a child with a high fever or who may have been vomiting, an update on a leg pain, or a refusal to go to school. I looked at the pink notes, set priorities, and then began to take care of each one.

Hopefully I could count on the help of a nurse experienced in "triage." A triage nurse is trained to recognize the significance of the symptoms of an illness a parent describes. The triage nurse knows how to exhaust the possibilities of telephone advice.

My office rule was to have no patient waiting in an examining room until I had arrived at the office and to have no patient undressed and in a gown until I was about to enter the room. Have you ever waited for a doctor in a cool, air conditioned room without clothes for more than half an hour? Imagine what that is like for a mother with active, healthy children plus a sick one!

Besides taking care of a red throat or an aching belly, I had to pay attention to the dynamics of the parent-child dyad and to how the family functioned. My job was also to observe. There is only one kind of good medicine: one that includes family dynamics in addition to a thorough physical exam. We should not need a special education in "holistic med-icine." All doctors should practice holistic medicine, that is – be tuned in to the patient as a whole.

The bond between pediatrician and patient can heal as much as any medication. That connection often has roots during the child's first year of life when the pediatrician's advice and support is so important. I recall Julia, a young mother who used to be my patient and whose child I treated years later in my practice; our interaction illustrates what I want to describe. Picture a young mother who waited with her two-month-old baby in her arms in an examining room. When I walked in she received me with a big smile. I, too, was glad to see her, and I sensed that she trusted me. Julia was slim, of average height, with delicate facial features and blondish hair. She appeared relaxed in her casual attire. The baby's weight had already been checked by my nurse, and we knew that it was appropriate for the child's age and size. I began with a typical question, "How often does Peggy breast-feed?"

The mother, ecstatic, answered, "My Peggy wants to eat around the clock but last night she and I had six hours of sleep for the first time!"

This was two more hours of rest than she had previously been able to obtain. We had agreed to wait until the longer periods between feedings occurred naturally and our plan had paid off. Julia laid the baby on the examining table and removed some of her clothes. Before I started the physical examination, I talked to little Peggy in a soft voice. The baby listened. A responsive smile followed, and the two of us engaged in a dialogue of sounds that only she and I understood. For me, that was one of the milestones of the visit. The mother stood next to us, smiling with pride. After I completed my task, the mother began to dress her baby, but I noticed a change in her demeanor. She informed me of her concern.

"I have only three months' leave, and I need to go back to work in a month," she said. "I don't want to stop breastfeeding, what can I do?"

Teary eyed, she was worried about the transition from breast to bottle the baby needed to make. In addition, her health insurer only would pay for one routine visit every two months. But the next few weeks, before the authorized next visit, would bring unavoidable changes in the baby's feeding schedule. What if she needed to see me during that period, she asked.

I tried to reassure her of my help. "Julia, you will be able to come whenever you have doubts about your milk supply or any other question."

In fact, I would see her without charging her, or I'd mark it as a follow up visit which would cost less. Insurance used to pay for a child's monthly visits until age six months. But to save money they cut the number of visits and the length of time allowed for each visit. Those were among the first steps that led to the way medicine is practiced today – driven by an intent to cut and abbreviate doctors' visits.

Julia and I both agreed about her efforts to continue using mother's milk.

"Will you be able to extract and save your milk at work or will you have to extract and discard it?" I asked.

We talked about bottles, nipples, and also the possibility that the baby's father could help with some feedings. Mothers' hours of sleep are important too.

Behind all the nitty-gritty discussion of practical details was my awareness of the impending first separation of the mother from her child – a difficult time for any mother. I felt for her as she was going through moments I'd gone through with my children. Empathy moved me, and I needed to hold back my own tears. Our space had to be occupied by her feelings not mine. Yet I was reminded of how hard it was with Odile, my third child. I had only one month's leave after having worked non-stop for twenty years. With the first two children, it was not as difficult since I was a medical student in Argentina with available help. Many women in the United States are still waiting for their employers to give them a chance to breastfeed for the child's first six months. By law they are still allowed only a three months leave.

I planned to help Julia myself in this transition since I preferred not to bring in the, then new, "lactation specialists." I wanted to offer her my experience as a woman and as a doctor. She left the office able to face the coming changes with more confidence.

I think of another mother I treated during my years at DMA. Mrs. Filbert, a short, frail-looking woman with thick-framed glasses, who wore a dark dress, and said to me, "You have been recommended by my best friend who recently moved to London. Here is my problem. For the last six weeks, my baby daughter has refused her bottles and sucks only when asleep."

Mrs. Filbert addressed me with hesitation while holding her five-month-old baby. Her anxiety, I surmised, came from more than one source. She was still assessing my skills (her friend wasn't around to reassure her); she was worried about her baby's possible weight loss, and she wasn't sure of her own competence as a mother. I asked several questions. I found her child normal, and the weight, although low, was within normal limits. I suspected that the baby may have been force-fed by a well-intentioned sitter and that this may have been the reason for her refusal. This mother worked full-time and needed to leave her baby with sitters. Her husband did not assist with feeding and was not able to participate in the care of the child. Help she had received from her best friend was no longer available. I had to be gentle with her when I shared my thoughts or gave her suggestions.

"It would be best to change sitters," I said, "and for the moment, let the baby continue to feed in the same way. You will need to make changes slowly. Before you go to work and after you return, forget about other chores. Take time to set little Rona in your lap, and spoon-feed her. Give her a few half-full spoons of soft food, preferably home-made."

My hope was that the tasty food and the mother's warmth would reintroduce the baby to the pleasure of eating while reassuring the mother of her own abilities.

A week later, with a phone call, I learned that there had been success with the solid food. Two weeks later, during a follow-up visit, I learned that the baby had also begun to take bottles from the mother. I saw the satisfaction of her success in the mother's eyes. I reminded her, "This baby is built like you and probably will not be a big eater. This is something anybody feeding her should remember."

This is the kind of success pediatricians hope for. It speaks about the importance of supporting the working mother, who needs to be validated and released from self-blame.

When the patient is the child of a working couple and both participate in the care of the baby, my support for them as a unit, and as individuals, is equally important. Since I began seeing patients at DMA in the 70's, I was witness to changes in the lives of couples as a consequence of the women's liberation movement. In particular, I saw the greater participation of men in what were traditionally women's tasks at home. Jerry and Nina were teachers, typically middle-class, who managed the care of their child and their home. Their handsome baby grew without incident and eventually they decided to move to another state. During their farewell visit I asked them the secret of their successful partnership. Jerry answered, "We always leave the sink empty and clean for each other." They respected each other's time and the fatigue that came with being a working parent.

Facing a different patient, I asked myself, "Who is in charge of eight-year-old Gilbert?" Gilbert was a slim child of average height, with brown hair and eyes. I saw him frequently for minor ailments. When his father brought Gilbert in one day with a sore throat, I asked him, "When did he start complaining? Did he have a fever? Did Gilbert take any medicines?" The father would then turn to the child and repeat my question because he did not know the details of his son's life. When, instead, the mother drove Gilbert to my office with a "belly ache" that obliged him to leave school that day, she, too, was unable to answer any of my questions. "What did he eat the day before?" or "For how long has he been in pain?"

If I asked, "Did he have a fever?" she would ask the child, "Did your father check you for a fever last night?" Children age eight don't usually remember much of what they ate or when they last pooped. I realized that neither of his parents was in charge of this child, and I decided it would be useful to discuss this with them. It was a fruitful meeting. They recognized that neither one of them felt responsible for their child's well-being. The child felt this, and it contributed to his illness. Gilbert showed signs of "functional symptoms." These are triggered by stress in children as they are in adults and may present as headaches and stomach pains that signal other problems. Both parents worked and neither had assumed caring for child's needs. As the years went by and more women joined the working force full time, increasingly, parents realized that one of the members of the couple needed to be in charge of their children. Or, if parents shared these responsibilities, then they needed to communicate.

Two of my patients were Irish beauties. Maria, the older, was more reserved. Her sister, Shauna, three years younger, competed for attention, aware of what a charming smile she had. When Shauna was barely three and a half, she began telling her mom that she had a headache. It went away quickly without any medicine and was soon forgotten. A few days later, she repeated her complaint. Was this a way to catch her mom's attention? Or, the mother wondered, might the child have a real medical issue?

In one of the family's visits to my office, the mother mentioned the child's complaint and her own doubts. Shauna's physical exam was normal as were her vision and her neurological exam. I did not want to order tests. However during the course of a visit ten days later, I saw Shauna raise her little hand and hold it to her head briefly. That was enough to refer her without delay to the neurosurgeon, who in turn diagnosed that Shauna had a small obstruction in the system of fluid that circulated around her brain. She was operated on and the symptoms disappeared. Headaches can be present in children frequently as symptoms of stress, but they are not common at Shauna's early age.

Today, less emphasis is placed on regular check-ups. That's unfortunate because knowing your patients when they are healthy helps you to recognize disease and assess its severity when they become unwell. For example, Betty was an active four year old who usually entered my office jumping. One day she came in in her father's arms. She had vomited and run a high fever the previous night and had not slept well. When lying on the examining table, she showed no interest in her surroundings. Normally Betty was a curious child. Just by looking at her I suspected she might have a significant infection. The father said that they had not noticed other symptoms, like a cough or a complaint of pain.

Betty was up-to-date in her immunizations. I examined her and did not find a focus of infection, but I noticed a flaring of her nares at the openings of her nose. The x-rays confirmed my suspicion of early pneumonia. A blood test helped me with the choice of antibiotics, and I gave proper care advice to the family. I followed Betty closely and expected a fast recovery.

Earaches and colds are common sources of complaint. Once children begin to socialize and come in contact with other children, they begin to experience viral upper respiratory infections, the common "colds." As the nose drips, fluid may accumulate in the middle ear and bacterial infections add to the effects of the virus. I can't count how many of those cases I have seen or how many telephone calls about them I received day or night from concerned parents. During the early years of my practice, we went back to the office in the middle of the night, in any weather, to take care of an ear infection.

Harry's was a typical example. Harry, a two-year-old blond with blue eyes, long eyelashes and an endearing way of looking at you, was also precocious. When I entered the examining room, he was sitting on his father's lap.

"What do you say?" his father said to him.

"Ay, Doc Styol!" answered Harry, smiling and expecting to hear praise.

My answer to Harry's greeting plus the few medical questions, took most of the ten minutes allowed by managed care for his visit. So I needed to take additional time since I knew that Harry's past ear infections had triggered episodes of asthma. Aware of this, his parents brought him to see me the morning after Harry had had a painful night. Harry sat quietly and cooperated. I turned the medical routine of observing his ear drums into a peekaboo game, gently placing my otoscope in each ear and I also listened to his chest. I found a red, moderately bulging eardrum and a low-grade fever. Then, the recommendations from the American Academy of Pediatrics suggested I should not prescribe antibiotics except in the case of a severe ear infection.

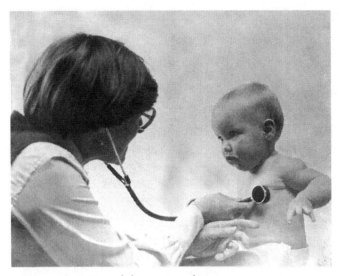

Luisa with her patient during an exam

What was I to do? This infection, severe enough to cause pain, could be followed by another of Harry's bouts of asthma. I never believed in prescribing a decongestant although that would have sent the father home satisfied with some medication for his child. Instead, I chose one of the well-established antibiotics reserving the newest medications for more serious illnesses. I suggested a follow up appointment to confirm that the infection resolved. Physicians were encouraged by insurers to cut down on follow-up visits. I ignored this dictate. Why? I found it imperative to rule out the chance of a prolonged hearing loss at a crucial time in the speech development of a toddler. I have lived through many, sometimes conflicting, changes in medicine, but I could not ignore what years of experience had taught me. The father did not leave without asking about my own health and that of my family, a gesture not unusual among my patients. Harry's ear infection resolved this time without consequences.

Even if an earache is the only complaint, I found a more thorough exam of the child is good practice. In recent years however, additional time constraints have been imposed on pediatricians so the exam is usually limited to only the organ related to the complaint.

When our office had been in the old Cape Cod-styled chalet, a young, attractive woman with an assertive attitude brought in five-year-old, Estelle, who was crying and complained that both her ears hurt. It was their first visit to me. The mother spoke English with a strong accent, and we soon embarked on an easy dialogue in Spanish. I still remember Estelle standing next to her mother, in pain, her head full of curls and her dark brown eyes questioning me. I overcame her reluctance to be examined and saw two infected ear drums. But I went on with my routine and listened to her heart and her lungs. As I started to feel her belly, my hand touched something hard in the space where I usually would be able to feel her liver and her bowel. I knew instantly that this was not the case of a simple ear infection. Estelle needed to have her abdomen examined using the sophisticated techniques that were available at The Children's Hospital. I had to communicate my findings, though in vague terms, to Estelle's mother. I explained that it would be wise to go for a consultation without delay. She listened to me, frowning, but did as had I advised.

What followed was a long, two-pronged fight for the child's life. The first part involved radiation and surgery, performed by a medical team from the Children's Hospital, to treat a cancerous growth found in Estelle's kidney. Working closely with the specialists and nurses at The Children's Hospital was one of my biggest privileges.

The second battle was one the mother had to wage at work with a famous Boston insurance company which did not want to allow her the time needed to take her daughter for treatments. The mother was divorced and financially dependent on her job. She had forged her courage fighting an authoritarian Cuban government and had suffered jail time for her efforts. Now she had to use her determination to battle for her daughter's care. She got up at dawn ready for the earliest available appointments for outpatient chemo or radiation treatments. My Latino background and our common language provided me with extra tools to support her.

Estelle survived and the family moved to Florida, but her mother still visited me occasionally. Years later, a good-looking woman in her twenties asked my secretary to see me. It was Estelle. She looked splendid.

In 2002, Tim came for his appointment, presenting a more benign situation than Estelle, but a multifaceted one. Tim was a chubby one-and-a-half year old boy with blue eyes. He was a third-generation patient of mine, a member of a gentle, dear family. His developmental milestones had been within normal limits but he had had several ear infections, and he cried incessantly during his first year of life. He cried every time he saw me. I was never successful in establishing a relationship with him. One day, Tim arrived and with the help of my nurse, who held him. I confirmed another ear infection and was ready to treat it. I stopped the mother to ask how many words Tim could say and found out that he had not added more than two or three since his recent fifteen-months check. So the most important issue for his visit that day shifted to his delayed speech.

In Massachusetts, hearing tests were done at birth, but I wondered if this situation didn't call for another one. Had Tim's recurrent ear infections impaired his hearing? Another hearing test would be done, but I also wondered if his parents encouraged him to talk? Did he have any cognitive impairment? All these issues could be evaluated by a program called "Early Intervention" which provides diagnostic services by doing observations at home. The program also provided treatment of developmental delays for children up to three years of age. Would the mother accept my referral? It happens often that if a parent fears anything is wrong with a child, the parent may deal with it with denial.

I chose my words carefully when I said to the mother, "You have been a good mother and tried really hard to avoid the colds that brought on Tim's ear infections. But I would like to also be sure that Tim is hearing well and that he is able to repeat your words. He will need a hearing test. In addition, there are specialists who can encourage Tim to talk and teach you how to help him. I will put you in touch with them."

I described the Early Intervention program and the mother had a positive attitude. She was glad for the two referrals which gave her new hope. They did help, but the pace of Tim's improvement was slow. His hearing was normal but he was diagnosed as having difficulties in social recognition. These were addressed as well.

Before computers, I had to do verbal referrals to auxiliary institutions for programs like "Early intervention." Often the lines to reach those institutions were busy, and I had to go through complicated switchboards. Referrals took a lot of my time, but I could not renounce my role as the coordinator of the team caring for these patients, and my time was rewarded by the parent's confidence and the patient's progress.

Jeffrey was a large eight-month-old baby with light colored eyes and blondish hair who, like Tim, also had an unusual number of ear infections. Jeffrey's failed to respond to treatment. He was the first born of two young parents and had been my patient since birth. My trained eye noticed something that troubled me about his large size, but initially I could not define the issue. I consulted with my associate David Winter who suggested a special urine test. I was astonished when it came back positive. Jeffrey's urine contained an abnormal amount of mucopolysaccharides, now referred to as glycolsaminglycans, because he had been born missing the enzyme that split these molecules and allowed for their normal metabolism. These compounds accumulated in many organs of his body, whereas normally they would contribute to their normal structure. I went once more to my favorite book of pediatrics and with heartbreaking pain, I learned about my patient's future. Dr. Winter's sagacious diagnosis had to be communicated to his parents. I decided to have a specialist confirm the ominous prognosis. I accompanied the parents to see Dr. Allan Crocker at The Children's Hospital, a caring doctor with considerable experience in rare diseases like this one. He confirmed the diagnosis of Hurler's syndrome and told these parents what to expect. He described, according to a medical tradition of total disclosure, the full impact of the malady. It would affect Jeffrey's appearance; his whole body would be different from other children's as he continued to grow. There was no known treatment.

It was such a painful session for the parents that they refused to believe Dr. Crocker or to ever see him again. Jeffrey lived for sixteen years, and I was the one who consulted with Doctor Crocker when we needed to. I had to witness the slow deformation of Jeffrey's face. His head became larger, especially from front to back. His forehead bulged, the nasal bridge depressed, and the front of the nose became more prominent. His features grew more coarse, and resembled the gargoyles of old Medieval churches, which is why the disease is also called "gargoylism." Despite his appearance, Jeffrey was a charmer with a pleasant manner toward the people around him. He attended special programs and went to kindergarten in a public school. Later, cognitive delays made it necessary for him to attend special schools. I shared the constant distress of Jeffrey's mother who was trying to fight a reluctant school system and at the same time obtain the constant medical care her son required. Jeffrey's bones and his trachea were the most critically affected. The bones failed to hold the frame of his body. He developed scoliosis and ended up in a wheel chair. The walls of the trachea, the tube that carried air to his lungs, became soft. so that later on, he needed a tracheostomy (an opening of the trachea to allow air in and out). He died at sixteen, more than twenty-five years ago. I vividly remember even the date of his funeral and the family's telephone number, which I had to dial frequently to support his brave mother. I still receive a card from her on holidays and updates on her healthy daughter.

During the time I treated Jeffrey, I also taught in a revolutionary program at Tufts School of Medicine in Boston. The program encouraged first year students to discuss clinical cases and obliged them to think, study and comment on psychological and socioeconomic considerations that might affect their patients. Jim, one of the students, declared that the "problem learning" class, as we called it, was pointless. Jim was going to be an orthopedic surgeon and he was sure that he would not need to deal with anything more than orthopedic issues. With Jim's objections in mind, I asked Jeffrey's mother to agree to bring Jeffrey and his x-rays to one of our program sessions. Jeffrey's kind nature facilitated the students' interviews, but Jim in particular became interested in Jeffrey and in his extensive orthopedic needs. Jeffrey's visit caused Jim to reconsider his "pragmatic" approach, which otherwise would have ignored important aspects of this patient as a human being.

Spring is a lovely time for many but not for those whose allergies exacerbate their problems. As a result, during the spring we often worked through the lunch break, and it was during one of those times that we received a call from a parent whose asthmatic child had a sudden increase of symptoms. Lunch time or not, we urged the parent to bring the child in without delay. David, a ten-year-old asthmatic, was pale and breathing faster than normal when he arrived. He appeared apprehensive when we asked how he was feeling. But he could talk with ease and answered our questions in detail. We evaluated the level of oxygen in his blood, measured the number of respirations and blood pressure and listened to his lungs. His breathing difficulty could have had repercussions on his heart. We needed rule out infection. His well prepared father came with the relevant information on David's medications. That allowed us to hook David to a nebulizer and add more medication. Next, he was observed and repeatedly evaluated. Would he respond to intensive treatment? If not, we would need to take David to the E.R. to receive more intense care or to be admitted. Fortunately David improved after two treatments and we found no indication of infection. I ordered x-rays to make sure the asthma was not complicated by an infection, and David went home with additional medications. We agreed to monitor his condition with repeated phone calls until the next day's visit.

Patients like David benefit from a close follow-up even when the child is not acutely ill. It helps them avoid emergency room visits and hospital admissions and allows us to better consider the many factors that may trigger the patient's crisis. My years at the Respiratory Institute in Argentina helped me understand the intimate details of patient lung pathology and motivated me to constantly update myself on new treatments. It also made me sensitive to their risks.

In addition to taking care of illnesses, I considered routine patient check-ups an important part of my work. These periodic assessments, required by the local public schools in those days, were an important instrument not only to follow up on an illness, but also to appraise the child's development, his adjustment to school and society, and to observe the family dynamics. I read that now, to save expenses, these visits are replaced in some school districts by reports written by the parents – even in populations where more surveillance is called for because of the family's economic difficulties.

The value of these encounters is illustrated by the story of Kevin, a fourth grader. I looked at his growth chart and saw that since his last visit a year ago, his weight gain had been poor.

"Does he eat his meals?" I asked the mother in our brief interview before my exam.

"He does not like the school food, and he often brings back what I prepare for his lunch," she answered.

Then I asked Kevin, "How is school this year?"

He replied, "My teacher does not like me."

The mother, noticing my interest in the school situation added, "His grades are only fair this year, and he refuses to play sports as he did before. That makes his father mad."

After the mother left the room, I examined Kevin and found no abnormalities other than the weight loss and his sad demeanor. I had taken care of him since birth and I suspected that something was troubling him and affecting his performance at school.

When I asked him, "Do you have a best friend?" he became teary and said, "It used to be Paul, but now he joined with the others."

"Who are the others? What do they do?" I asked.

"Are you going to tell my parents?" Kevin immediately asked, with a worried expression. But without giving me time to answer, he rushed to tell me, "They make fun of how I walk; they don't talk to me now, and they grab my lunch when they have a chance. I'm always afraid of what they will do next and I feel stupid."

I promised that I would find a way out of this situation and explained that what was happening was not Kevin's fault. They were bullying him because they were dealing with their own insecurities. I tried to reassure him that if I explained this to his parents, they would be on his side.

I asked the mother and child to return with the father, and they scheduled an appointment, reputedly to talk about their child's weight loss. After a meeting with the parents and the child, I planned to follow up with a visit to school to talk with the teacher. I was a pediatrician, but I knew my task shouldn't have ceased at the end of a stethoscope.

Bullying is part of the spectrum of violence from child to child that I saw in my office, and I could not ignore it. A firm and appropriate intervention by the school and some therapeutic support for my patient would improve the situation. Kevin's case was one example of the many times I intervened to stop interpersonal violence when I saw it affecting my young patients. Today, bullying and its consequences are recognized as serious social problems – at long last.

Charlie was ten years old. His mother was in the waiting room and when asked, she said she had no questions for me. Charlie answered all my questions and reported that his school grades were good and that he was playing baseball this season. His team was doing well. All the parameters I could measure pointed to a healthy child. This straightforward visit was common but important as it provided another link in the patient's history and a basis for comparison that might be useful in the future.

Twelve-year-old Mirella's was my next scheduled check-up. She was sitting on the examining table and already wearing one of our patient's gowns made of a cheery fabric. Before I entered the room, I looked at her growth chart, and I noticed a jump in her weight not in proportion to her growth in height. A red flag! Two years had passed since her last checkup. Mirella's weight was always slightly above her ideal for her age, but never in the excess it was. She was in a good mood and cooperative. Her thick dark hair dark fell in waves, framing a round, expressive face. I recognized the areas where she applied makeup with precocious ability on her white skin.

"How is school going this year?" I asked.

"Better than last year," she said.

"Are you playing any sports?"

"I don't like team sports. I go to the pool," she says.

When I examined her I felt her neck, and I checked the size and softness of her thyroid. I checked her pulse rate and began to rule out hormonal problems. When I finished my examination, I asked her to get dressed and asked her mother back in. A few minutes later, I found myself in the presence of a, frankly, obese woman. Despite an exam without any signs of disease, I asked for blood tests to rule out hypothyroidism. I suspected I'd find myself facing a frequent challenge: to encourage them to break a familiar cycle of obesity without hurting the feelings of parents or patient. It's always a family effort to implement changes in the eating habits of a child.

Initially, I asked my patient to write down what the child ate and drank for three days and then to return for a follow up-visit with the information. Mirella's was the second case that day for which I scheduled "an after 5 p.m. meeting" to address the children's eating habits with the parents. Obesity became an epidemic that stretched the resources of the American health system.

Check-ups also have allowed me to find unexpected skin cancers, kidney diseases without apparent symptoms, thyroid dysfunction, hidden bowel inflammations, and above all, a chance to follow the physical and mental development of my patients. Pediatrics is all about prevention.

To honor an obligation to share my experience with the next generation of students, just as doctors before had shared with me, I received students from Harvard University and Tufts University School of Medicine. They came to spend time with me and to learn about the real world of the pediatrician, outside the academic world of the teaching hospital.

One of the students, a young woman eager to learn, spent a day in my office. Like me she was short. A thick braid of dark hair fell on her back and contrasted with her white doctor's jacket. The name of her well-known university was on the front of her jacket, and reassured my patients. The medical student followed me through earaches and routine checkups, learning about bedside manners and long term patient-doctor relationships. My patients often eased her encounters by offering positive comments. Occasionally, for reasons of privacy, a patient would refuse her presence in the examining room. At one point, what had seemed a routine day, became anything but routine with Helen's case. Helen was a sixteen-year-old who called for an appointment complaining of abdominal pain.

That kind of complaint was a red flag for my secretary who knew the patient would need extra time. The patient would also be asked to fill out a questionnaire while waiting for me. I usually reviewed the questionnaire with my patient and asked more questions so as not to miss any information.

The morning of Helen's appointment, I walked into the examining room and found Helen stripped of her street clothes and wearing the customary gown, sitting on a chair. She was blond, of medium height, light weight, with brown eyes and a gentle smile. She had given permission for the medical student to be present during the first part of her visit while she gave the reason for her visit. She'd felt pain in her lower abdomen for the last two months. The pain was dull, not severe, but it did not go away. Together we reviewed her answers and I added new questions about her menses. When I examined her, I easily found a hard tumor in the area where she had felt pain. Aware that I could be dealing with an unusual problem, I casually asked her, "Did you drive yourself here?"

Helen answered, "Yes, my mother's breast cancer is back, and she is not feeling well enough to drive because of her new treatment. I did not want to add to her worries so I did not call you earlier."

I had known Helen's mother for many years, and I was acquainted with her devotion to her child. I ordered a few tests in my office. Helen waited for the results, but they were not sufficient for me to make a firm diagnosis. I had found a tumor, and I had to explain to my young patient that doctors use that word to refer to any mass. It did not necessarily mean the tumor was malignant. I added, "Your mother eventually will find out about your medical appointments, and she will worry more not knowing the reason for them. It would be better if you explained everything to her. I'll be glad to talk to her too."

Helen listened, thought for a moment and agreed with me. As I talked to her, I was aware that I would have to be available and supportive as I followed her diagnosis and in turn made the necessary referrals. More tests and treatments were called for, though I would not necessarily be the physician who would order them. The medical student observed and saw how isolated the practitioner can be taking the steps that could lead to a more complicated diagnosis. The physician bears the responsibility for the ultimate care of the patient as well as how the family reacts to it.

Fortunately in Helen's case, it turned out that the tumor was a congenital benign tumor, diagnosed with the help of, and removed by, the expert surgeon to whom I had referred my patient. Helen's mother was able to see her daughter recover completely from the surgery before she herself succumbed to breast cancer.

Research scientists may dream of a Nobel Prize, but what laurel crown can we pediatricians hope for? The answer: only humble prizes but they are no less significant. I'll describe three of them that occurred in a single week.

First, I entered the examining room where one-and-half-year-old Paul waited with his mother and father. All were happy to see me. Children at this age can be difficult to examine, and some may perceive our examination as aggression. I felt relief when I was greeted by a smiling Paul, and I was moved when Paul began to cry when I left the room. More often than not, it is just the reverse; a child cries when the pediatrician walks into the room.

The second wonderful thing to happen occurred when I saw a four-year-old boy from a Lebanese immigrant family still struggling to adjust to American culture. During the family's visits to my office, I had taken the time to validate their approach to Fadi's care. Fadi had come often since he, his brother and cousins had a case of "ping-pong" strep. The infection kept going from one child to the others. During one of his first visits, still unable to express himself in English, Fadi turned to his father and asked him to invite me to their home. More recently, when his father asked him, "What do you want to be when you grow up?" he answered, "Dr. Stigol."

And finally the third reward. Rose, almost three, a blond haired, blue-eyed beauty sat in her mother's lap while I examined her. Her father was also in the office, holding Rose's brother on his lap. Before I started my exam, the mother told me that the little boy had been looking forward all day to this visit. These soft-spoken parents treated their children with a tenderness that matched the children's thin, small bodies. This entirely harmonic picture was very different from the scene on their last visit - the desperate screaming children in my office only a few months ago. They had repeated colds and fevers, caught in day care, and it was a dramatic event each time I had to look in their ears and throat. During my examination this time, Rose turned to her mother, and referring to me, said, "She is a nice person."

When I finished the exam she extended her arms to me and said, "Now I need a hug."

She repeated the request before she left. I could not help but think back to the many times that they were in my office screaming. I rejoiced at the turn of events.

Patients may reward us also with their confidence as they grow up, asking us to advise them on sensitive issues. Adolescents represent a real challenge to the doctor just as they often do to their parents. Hormones change their bodies and produce upheavals that impact how they view their family and their world. These changes often come with an intensity of feelings that can trigger socially unacceptable behavior or physical (somatic) symptoms of illness. Sometimes they are vague and hard to define. Other times they are more precise, like a shortness of breath, abdominal pains, or headaches. The physician has to trust his or her clinical experience while considering the emotional origin of the symptoms. Tests may confirm a patient's fear of being sick, but at the same time, the physician needs to be sure not to miss an organic problem. The first step of a diagnosis is to question the patient, but this is also difficult with adolescents, often inclined not to share the cause of their distress or a private detail of their lives. They may perceive their doctor as a friend, but they can also see him or her as part of the very "establishment" with which they are in conflict. Aside from these considerations, adolescents are old enough to develop an illness related to internal medicine, obliging their doctor to consider a whole new array of diseases. Addictions can start in this confusing time when individual reevaluation and peer pressure influences are the rule.

Brian was a twenty-year-old who chose to remain in my practice. I had taken care of him and his four siblings for many years. He was tall but thin and was eating less than usual. He described a frequent acid reflux from his stomach. I examined him and felt a larger than normal liver. The rest of the examination was normal. Blood tests showed that Brian's liver enzymes were higher than normal, confirming what I found in my physical exam. We discussed his diet and habits, and he admitted to a significant alcohol intake. Because the amount he was drinking was not so unusual among his friends, he was not aware that this was a problem. He accepted my referral to a specialized psychologist, and I hoped he would follow through on it.

During a routine checkup, Sixteen-year old Earl admitted that his grades were falling. When we discussed the reasons for it, alcohol again appeared as the probable cause. Earl mentioned his father's drinking, and I realized that this was a family problem. I needed to approach it as such. The father came and explained to me that his goal was to teach his child how much alcohol Earl could ingest and not create an embarrassing social situation. The father would not agree to a no-alcohol policy. I worried about my patient's future but felt powerless.

An abusive father's alcoholism was behind the frequent physical ailments and bouts of depression of four siblings who came to my office for many years. I did not learn about the father's alcoholism until finally the mother, a quiet woman with a permanent smile on her face, described the cruel reality of their lives. Alcohol, like violence, is a carefully hidden secret in many families. I would not have suspected that this gentle, short man who held a responsible job in the community could be responsible for the abusive behaviors she described.

More than once I feared for patients who had been driven to see me by a parent who smelled of alcohol and who had the acid breath that is the telltale sign of it. Even when confronted in the most supportive terms about the risks they were exposing their children to, they always denied their condition.

Denial could go a long way. I had taken care of Tony since he was a toddler. His mother spoke in a low voice, and she seemed very concerned about Tony and his younger brother. On one occasion, Tony came for his fourteen-year-old for a routine checkup. He was clearly depressed. He had failed to gain weight, and at his age, this would mean he would not grow to the expected height. As we began to talk about my findings, he admitted to a deep craving for alcohol. I can still see him sitting in front of me, bent over and holding his head, with tears filling his deep blue eyes. I rushed to find a treatment program for a boy of his age group. My search was successful, and I made a phone referral to Boston Children's Hospital where he could be seen soon. At least I knew that when I went to talk to Tony's mother, I could offer a problem with a possible solution. Her reaction was unexpected. She adamantly refused our advice, and later I realized that she had also disappeared from my practice.

High risk behaviors in adolescents are an important topic in the field of pediatrics. We often encounter addictions, sexual issues, driving issues, and risk-taking attitudes that can be deleterious. Unfortunately I saw many patients who illustrated the point. They stand out in my memory; some who died in a car or a motorcycle accident during their adolescence. I cannot forget them.

The intense feelings of the adolescent can make them perceive life as a drama, and sometimes they are the protagonists in those dramas. I was the pediatrician for three lovely sisters whose mother was a friendly and talkative person. Communication with her seemed easy. One of her daughters, Renee, came to see me one autumn day, complaining of abdominal pains. She was a tall adolescent of average weight and much less communicative than her mother. Before the physical exam, she filled out a standard questionnaire with information about her bowel movements, diet and menses that did not provide any clues. Since the physical exam did not show abnormalities, I asked her again about her school performance and whether she had any problems at home or with her friends. "No" was her short answer to all my questions. I suggested a new diet, asked her to keep track of her bowel movements when on that diet and told her to come back in two weeks. If that didn't solve the problem, then I would have her tested. When she did not return, I assumed her symptoms were gone. One unforgettable spring day, however, the terrible news reached me. She had been found lying on the floor of her home with a bullet in her head. She used one of her father's guns – a pediatrician's nightmare.

Adolescents have to deal with their intense sexual drive in a chaotic society that permits behaviors but doesn't prepare children who act upon them. Some parents are intent upon controlling sexual needs. Others find it easier to ignore them. A few recognize the strong pull of their children's peers in determining how they behave. Some parents are ready to join the adolescent's roller-coaster ride and always be available to them. The pediatrician tries to help educate patients, but our own experiences invariably influence how we handle them.

I dealt with my own sexual urges by getting married at eighteen. I also lived in a society that did not accept sex before marriage. I knew then less than a nine-year-old knows today even though I was a medical student. I don't recommend such ignorance. Yet some parents still insist on keeping sex a taboo subject with their teenagers.

I copied a questionnaire from a seminal publication, the *Pediatric Clinics of North America*, that was supposed to make interviews about sexuality easier for an adolescent to endure. The first patient I handed the suggested questions to while waiting to see me happened to be a girl who was a new patient. Her mother became so indignant with the mention of birth control and drugs in the questionnaire that they never returned.

For a large number of parents, denial is the best way to avoid facing certain behaviors in their children. Of course, the children do not stop those behaviors, but the parents have cut off a means of communication that can be significant in supporting a teenager at risk.

Some mothers, of course, demonstrated a more positive attitude. They asked my help in approaching their adolescent daughters on the difficult subject of sex, aware that societal parameters change and afraid that their child's ignorance might result in sickness or an unwanted pregnancy. Many of my patients, however, had already made up their minds on the subject and did not want to discuss their position. I still remember the mother of an eighteen-year-old who asked me to begin talking to her daughter about sex. When I shared her mother's concern, my patient, who had been reticent with me in the past, said, "I have had sex with the same guy for the last four years. I know how to take care of myself."

Some pediatricians prescribed birth control pills, but I believed that a young woman who is sexually active needed to be under the care of a gynecologist. To preserve the young person's privacy, I would find some reason for a referral. With young men, I took the time to talk about signs of sexually transmitted diseases and to discuss the notion that oral sex is safer.

An anorexic patient came to see me for a banal sore throat. Upon examining her I found a very fast pulse. Her heart was beating rapidly to compensate for her reduced circulating blood volume, a sign that she needed immediate attention. Unfortunately, anorexia is encouraged by our absurd fashion standards. It took many years for the public and for schools to recognize eating disorders are a serious health threat.

Very often pediatricians need to be social workers. A single mother brought me her 12 year old boy for a first visit. Both he and his mother were shy. She seemed sorry to be taking up my time. Both had a pleasant smile, rich dark hair and slightly slanted eyes, having come from the Philippines. At the next checkup, a year later, the boy said a few more words, and I learned about his poor self-image. It gave me a chance to talk to him. The following year, the mother spoke to me about her efforts, working at two jobs, and the child's anger about being left every afternoon and even on some weekends, with a sitter he disliked. His school performance deteriorated. I asked her more about her background. She had been a nurse in her native country but was working at present in jobs below her level of training, and it made her feel inferior. We discussed the important opportunity she was missing by not spending more time with her child, her need to find work that was more appropriate given her educational background, and the effect all of this would have on her child. By the next year, she had found a way to go back to school. She had updated her degree and was now a nurse in a psychiatric clinic with big responsibilities – and fewer hours. The child's self-esteem was much higher. He was more outgoing, and they enjoyed the extra time they spent together.

I have also seen many children who, during difficult times in their life, made a choice to overcome difficult circumstances. Several knew how to take advantage of a supportive family and worked steadily towards the goal of a productive life. The pediatrician becomes a proud witness to the maturing process of these teenage patients.

In 1973, when I began working full-time at DMA, there were no neonatologists at Newton-Wellesley Hospital. We were called in if the delivery of a baby might prove difficult or if it required our immediate attention. I remember rushing to the hospital on a snowy day, spinning my tire in traffic on Rte. 128, or speeding in the middle of the night along the deserted highway. A few years later the hospital built a model neonatology unit with its own intensive care facility. Dr. Clement Smith, who I had met during my first visit to Boston in 1962, was the pioneer in the field of neonatology, and he was responsible for building up that specialty in Boston. Through his work, many infants who were either severely premature, or in danger for other reasons could now be treated. I will always remember that when I had first met this great man, the Children's Hospital had only one room for him and his assistant, Dr. Steve Cochran.

In more ordinary cases, taking care of the first newborn in a family was a new adventure, not only for the parents but often in some ways for me. It was an opportunity to use my experience as a doctor but also as a mother. Ideally, I would have a meeting with the parents in my office a few weeks before the delivery. But more often I met the mother or the parents for the first time in the cold atmosphere of the hospital, where the pressure of the institution's schedule, and often my own, had to be considered.

I knocked at the door, disturbing Mrs. Beckett who had delivered her child only a few hours earlier. I found her snoozing and greeted her with a, "Good morning, I'm doctor Stigol, and I was asked to see your baby."

"Oh yes", the sleepy mother answered, "The Jones' recommended you."

Her baby boy was asleep in his crib near her bed. Being born is a shock to the infant's body. The new being must leave the mother's womb and face a much cooler environment. Birth requires that the little body undergo drastic physiological changes, like getting rid of fluid in the lungs and beginning to fill them with air. The boy I visited was recovering, well wrapped so as to survive the sudden transition from the warmth of the mother to the excessive air conditioning of the hospital room.

Newborn faces can also be very expressive. Mrs. Beckett's baby had a nice pink face and the posture of his arms and legs, gently bent, as well as the face, were all in a state of normal relaxation. He was breathing regularly. I did not see the intermittent pattern of faster and slower breathing that infants have on occasion and that usually disappears in a couple of weeks. I dared to touch him, and he seemed aware of it. I gently moved his limbs, listened to his heart and lungs, and felt his abdomen. Using the light of an ophthalmoscope, I examined his eyes – without any cooperation from my patient. Mrs. Beckett could not wait any longer and she asked, "Doctor, does he have all his parts? Are they all okay?"

"Yes," I answered, "he is a beautiful, normal baby."

When I finished my exam, I asked the mother, "How are you planning to feed your baby?"

She said, "I would like to breastfeed but I don't have any family to help, so it might be difficult for me."

I told her that breastfeeding was as old as man on earth, and I promised to help her during the demanding first weeks.

"I breastfed my three children even though I was studying or working at the same time," I explained.

Throughout my years of practice I have helped many women learn to breastfeed, and I prefer to act as the "lactation specialist" myself if the mother does not have another preference.

Ideally, a discussion about the baby's circumcision would have taken place in my office during the prenatal visit with the parents. I asked about their decision and learned that the baby would be circumcised later that day. I liked to gather as much information as I could about the mother, including her mood and the amount of support she would have from other members of the family. This knowledge made the daily telephone advice I would give her more effective. I repeated the importance of communicating with me.

"Never stop calling with a question because you think that 'doctors are busy,'" I said.

She, feeling reassured, smiled.

If it were possible, I would observe her baby at her breast, but one way or another, I hoped that I left her feeling more relaxed than she was when I walked into the room.

When I finished the interview and was about to leave the nursery, one of the lead nurses asked me to see another baby whose mother spoke only Spanish. In those days, bilingual services were not available as they are today. Social Services was concerned because the mother acknowledged that she had been mistreated at times by the child's father. As a member of the Committee on Violence to Women of the Massachusetts Medical Society, I was expected to be familiar with recommendations and to support and advise this woman on the risks that she and her baby might face. My native Spanish facilitated the interview and she agreed to see me for the care of her newborn. She was breastfeeding him and breastfed babies often require frequent weight checks. The weight checks would also allow me to closely follow the family dynamic. A more confrontational approach could have put her at risk.

Our "hospital rounds" included visits to our patients who were admitted to the Children's Hospital. It was a privilege that I didn't take lightly. I liked to know the details of each case. My exchanges with the hospital residents team were important. The team often had the most current information on a disease or a new treatment approach, but I was likely to know more about the patient's past, or could add an observation from my years of experience.

After finishing hospital rounds, I returned to my office. Around the time of my retirement in 2005, patients' pediatric visits were replaced by the care of "hospitalists," selected and employed by the hospital. We communicated with them. Our presence in the hospital was not required. I see it as one more way in which our ties to our patients were lessened in the name of efficiency.

During the early eighties, significant changes affected the practice of medicine. The US government began to certify HMO (Health Maintenance Organizations) plans in 1977. HMOs began to curtail the independence of the practitioner. We were less the owner of our decisions when it came to the care of our patients. The patients were less able to choose their doctors. Our income no longer depended on a fee schedule that we had chosen or suggested. Fees were now up to third parties who decided what we were worth and how much time we would take with a patient. Clinicians became providers and typical commercial propaganda began to sell our product. When I graduated in Buenos Aires, in 1954, you would open your office and wait for your good name to bring you patients. It was frowned upon when my father had published a very small ad with his name and his specialty in a newspaper. We could not foresee what was coming. Once at the entrance of DMA, a life-size cartoon of a family was installed by the public relations department of one of the successive HMO's who swallowed our practice after several maneuvers to destroy it.

I committed myself to adhere to the high standards with which I was trained and those employed at the Harvard Children's Hospital – no matter what and despite these changes. I believed that my patients sensed my commitment, and, with my colleagues, we continued rendering the best quality services we could offer. The new systems and longer hours obliged us to share in this effort.

In 2005, after my struggle with ovarian cancer the year before, I resigned to leave the practice of medicine.

6

Personal and Family Life, 1973-80's

In remembering the part of my life when I lived in Dedham, I look back at the years when Odile was at school. Since the age of four, she had attended Dedham Country Day School, the kind of idyllic place that made you think that the world would be different if all children would have the opportunity to attend schools like this one. Here, children learned basic human values in addition to words and numbers. The wonder of those years was raising Odile with Florian. Odile was the center of our lives, perhaps the significant, positive aspect of my marriage.

We gave her music, ballet and skating lessons and ushered her through the early grades of her school, affectionately known as DCD. Odile learned to read recorder pieces before she learned to read books. Florian and I postponed evenings out until she went to boarding school at age 14. Her father and I were busy trying to fill gaps in the babysitter's schedules ourselves. Time free from work was set aside to be spent with her.

It is hard to believe now how difficult it was then to find after-school care. When Odile was admitted to DCD, they made it clear to me, in a stern way, that they would not tolerate any delay in picking her up. It was stressful to leave my office exactly on time, then sit at the end of a long line of cars waiting to pick up the children. A neighbor with a child in Odile's class helped on some days, and she would also feed Odile lunch. At one point, we had a live-in nanny who came to us with the greatest recommendations.

Her father had been a doctor, and this cultured woman was an opera lover with an impressive record collection. We could never understand why her children did not visit or invite her, until one day when she contracted the "flu" and asked me for cough medicine. In two days, she finished a large bottle of codeine syrup. I figured that if her system had been able to process such a large amount, she had to have a tolerance developed before this ingestion. Of course, it turned out she was an alcoholic who had managed to hide her habit. Once discovered, she got drunk day after day, and we had to have her removed from the house. It was – I thought – my first experience with alcoholism, a preview of the wrenching addiction. Odile was then in the second grade and was glad to see this woman leave. Pediatricians' office hours ended later than they do today, and it was hard to be home at a reasonable hour. Florian played squash at a downtown club many evenings unless I was on call. Still, to deal with Odile's schedule, I needed to be a juggler.

In 1977, Odile, nearly eight, and I went to Brazil to meet my father. It was a wonderful trip. My father, always so generous with me, still had some money as he'd continued to work. My brother, who had sophisticated taste, suggested a five-star hotel on the ocean in the southern part of Brazil. We were a large group consisting of my father, his wife and her niece Rachel who lived with them, my brother, his wife and three children, myself and Odile. Odile was close in age to one of my nieces. Florian refused to go. He disliked traveling other than going to Europe and even then he was reluctant to leave home. (I realized later what his attraction to staying home alone was. It provided Florian the opportunity to drink without interference.)

The Brazilian hotel's warm ocean with its bright colors and palm trees, the tropical fruits, and the best cuisine in the world, offered a setting not easily matched.

After our stay at the ocean, Odile and I went to Sao Paulo, where we visited a family we had met at the hotel. We also visited Cary Perry, an ex-patient of mine who was working with teen mothers in a poor area of the city. In later years, our paths crossed many times. I took care of Cary's children and trained Cary as a pediatric nurse practitioner. She also worked in the violence prevention project which I organized in 1990. (Years later, Cary was one of the speakers at my retirement party.)

Florian's father, Hellmuth, also invited us to join him and his wife on several memorable trips until his death in 1983. We traveled with them to Germany and to Bopard on the Rhine River. Traveling with Helmuth was special. He sang the "Lorelei" on our barge trip and was aware of the local geography and of cultural nuances. Traveling with him gave us a chance to admire his sketches. Because of those trips and as we also visited family in Europe and South America, Odile became a seasoned traveler at an early age.

Prior to my trip with Odile to Bopard, I was on call in Boston one night in 1976 when I answered a call from a child's mother whom I had not treated before. Suspecting a serious illness, I went to see the child in my office without delay. The little girl did not present any of the symptoms I expected to find, and after a thorough exam, I sent her home. The child had an airway obstruction and died the following day at The Children's Hospital. They found her to have a congenital blood condition that hastened the course of her illness. It was discovered after my exam which did not evidence any of the warning signs. Still, her death triggered a severe depression in me. I suggested that we, pediatricians, change procedures to avoid a similar event, but I found no support among my colleagues.

In 1978 I was sued. That, too, depleted my confidence. I began to question my decisions. Should I order more x-rays even if doing so would expose my young patients to more radiation? Was I properly weighing the benefits versus the risks of medications? Was I adjusting the dosage to exactly match the weight of each child? The pain due to the loss of this patient, only a year younger than my own daughter, seemed to be with me always. I was unable to face a jury, and the lawsuit was settled out of court.

In February of that same year, 1978, we, and several million other New Englanders, lived through what became known as "the blizzard of the century." As *The Boston Globe* described it:

> "A savage blizzard packing hurricane force winds dumped up to four feet of snow on many parts of Massachusetts, Rhode Island, and Connecticut between the 6th and 7th of February 1978. Not only did the deep snows paralyze highway traffic, but because of the mountainous waves it created during record high tides, hundreds of people were sent fleeing from their coastal homes, their houses reduced to rubble. Fifty-four died and highways and neighborhood streets alike were left clogged with abandoned, snow-covered vehicles. It was many days before community life returned to normal."

As the snow fell, I was often one of the last in our practice to leave. I recall that as the blizzard started I had to stay late to stitch the bleeding wound of a child. My car was buried in snow, and the father, who owned a truck, drove me home. Only police, firemen and doctors were allowed to drive on the few snow-cleared streets. I was the only woman allowed to drive in my town. We would make our way from home through a narrow path of snow that was taller than I was.

For five weeks the storm reduced everyone's activities. In my case, less work meant less income. That meant that when we thought about a summer vacation, we were short the money. Even so, Florian and Odile went to Europe in grand style and even visited my own friend in Kassel that summer. I can't help but think back on this and marvel at how often I would accept his behavior. I earned our income and paid our household expenses. Florian covered the extraordinary expenses like painting the house, and paid his own personal expenses with money his family sent him regularly. But thinking back, I was the one who needed the vacation most, and I was the one staying behind to work. I was too compliant. I should have demanded more consideration. But making those demands on Florian was not a part of my consciousness, and I went along with this expenditure.

In September 1978, my mother-in-law, Edith, died unexpectedly in Buenos Aires. Upon hearing that she was in a coma, Florian rushed to Argentina immediately. She was already dead when he arrived.

Edith had left him some money and possessions. Then two days later, her brother-in-law, who had also been sick, died in Buenos Aires. The two deaths brought Lilly, his wife and Edith's older sister, closer to us. Later Lilly invited us to travel to Switzerland with her and she visited us for successive summers.

Lilly had no children of her own. In later years, at age 89, she published a memoir of her years in Germany during the rise of Nazism. Florian helped edit it.

In 1979, Florian and I decided to move Odile from DCD to the more renowned Winsor School. We felt that Odile was not challenged enough and wanted a more demanding school. But the planned move upset Odile. For six weeks, before bedtime, she cried about missing DCD. I worried. Did we make the right choice? But after Odile's initial sadness, the Winsor School became an exciting experience for her as a student and for me as a parent. The Winsor School represented the formal and traditional education that Florian and I wanted for Odile. She thrived there academically, and on the surface, her life – and ours – appeared normal.

Florian and I took considerable pleasure in enjoying our beautiful home. Although short of money, Florian came home with fresh flowers every week and once in a while bought objects for our home. I bought, on monthly payments, two lavish Meissen flowerpots for the mantel piece of the dining-room.

We had dinner on a white tablecloth with matching napkins every night. We lit silver candlesticks and had a Japanese Imari centerpiece – the flower pots adding to the setting. But sadly, this beautiful setting could not prevent Florian's deep malady. Despite a lovely-two course dinner with two desserts and the best wine, Florian's depression deepened – the result of his alcoholism. More and more the alcohol spoke through him. He became increasingly negative about everything and was especially critical of our marriage. The result was that most evenings now ended with a cloud of sadness hanging in the air.

By 1983, Florian and I had been living in Dedham for a decade. I was well established as a local physician, and we were partially integrated into the community. We did not socialize a great deal. Florian played tennis with neighbors, and I took care of their children. However, the problems that had existed all along between us began to surface more frequently. By then I was aware that Florian was chronically depressed.

I worried; how I would deal with my depressed husband, an adolescent and a full-time job. Besides, the Winsor School was too conservative in style at that time. Odile brought up the idea of boarding school. Through one of my patients, I learned of the Emma Willard school in Troy, New York. Odile and I drove to visit it. We took secondary roads. An electric storm surprised us in the middle of a mountainous stretch, but we arrived and marveled at the setting of the school. Odile had an interview and was accepted to enter in the 10th grade.

Even now, years later, I become teary when I remember the anguish I felt when, in 1984, I left my youngest daughter at boarding school for the first time. She reassures me that it was a step that she chose. Still, I felt responsible. I was the one who could not cope with a depressed husband, and a child who was beginning to feel the pain of having an alcoholic father added to the emotional ups and downs of normal adolescence. My head had to be clear. I was treating patients and financially supporting my family. The life and death of the people I treated was in my hands. My responsibilities were huge.

Florian's aunt, Lilly, helped pay Odile's tuition, and I was in charge of her living and boarding expenses. I visited Odile at school often, in good and bad weather. I traveled the road by myself frequently, and on one of those trips, I had an accident that shook me although I was not badly hurt.

My shepherd dogs were a great pleasure. All of us loved them. They put an additional demand on us, but they were faithful and handsome companions. Often, after Odile went to boarding school, I'd arrive home late at night from a hospital visit. If our shepherd Daphne had not accompanied me, she would be the only one waiting to greet me. I would see the light in Florian's bedroom go off when he heard the sound of our big wooden gate, upon my arrival. He did not want contact with me because he had been drinking.

Meanwhile, at the age of 74, my beloved father was struck blind. The macular degeneration that he hadn't acknowledged but had coped with for years, had worsened and then left him blind. I noticed that his sight had decreased slightly before he lost it altogether. He had been working full time in the city and spending weekends at his "quinta." On one occasion, Odile and I visited him, and we joined my father and my stepmother on a trip to the quinta. On the drive back, I noticed the car was not properly aligned to enter a main, busy, two-way road. He was a cautious driver so I suspected his sight was impaired. The next day, I brought him to see a professor of ophthalmology, an old acquaintance of mine from the Hospital de Clinicas. He forbade my father ever to drive again. It represented a dramatic turn in my father's life.

Blind, he naturally had to stop working. He began to sell his few properties. He needed money, and I provided it, at first supplementing the income from the sale of his properties, and later paying for all his needs.

During one of my visits to see him in later years, I noticed a hole in the sole of his shoe. The next day we went to his favorite shoe store, and I bought him a new pair. How often in earlier years had he bought shoes for me and my children! The action made him sad.

He said, "When a father buys for a son, both smile; but when a son buys for a father, both cry."

I responded, "We will be the exception, and both of us will smile."

In 1986, Florian and I celebrated our 20th wedding anniversary. As his gift to me, I asked him to agree to go to therapy for his depression. I recommended a doctor I had seen when I was depressed after a patient died and who was my reserve when I needed help. I knew I would no longer be able to see him again if Florian was his patient. That was my gift to Florian. But the doctor did not address Florian's addiction until I went a few years later with Florian and raised the issue.

In 1987, during her summer vacation, Odile's concern for her father led to a meeting with a professional who confronted Florian and me with his drinking. Florian denied any problem and I agreed. How blind and ignorant about alcoholism I was. I imagine how Odile must have felt.

Odile graduated from Emma Willard in 1988. She had been accepted "early" at Vassar, her first choice among the 17 colleges we visited. We made a lovely small but memorable party for her at home. Florian's step-mother, Lesley, came from England to help us celebrate. Florian and I remained married, but not for long.

At about that time, Florian had an accident and totaled my car. It did not occur to me then that alcohol may have had a role. A few months later my secretary invited Florian and I to her home for an elegant dinner. Florian drank non-stop. When we returned home, he drove the car into the gate. It was blatant evidence that things were out of control.

Like most alcoholics, Florian drifted into and out of normal behavior. He took Odile to college that fall. On arrival, Odile did not want to stay at the college, but Florian convinced her to stay, and eventually she settled into college life. She soon had her first boyfriend. I hoped Odile would have a successful social life, but I also worried about the toll her father's alcoholism might have on her. After all, she could see my relationship with Florian was deteriorating by the moment. As the years progressed, Odile became more and more outspoken about the difficulties she was having with her father's drinking.

During all those years, I raised Odile as if she were an only child. But even though they weren't living with us, my older children were also a source of both pleasure and great concern. Georgina left home for college at Sarah Lawrence in 1968. It was the year of the Columbia students' upheaval, and she joined them. Georgina dropped out of Sarah Lawrence and lost her scholarship. She chose not to return to live with Florian and me. She returned to Argentina before Odile was born the following year. Georgina became a secretary for her grandfather, a famous psychiatrist, and tried to continue her studies. There she met the man who would become her husband. She had to leave Argentina in 1977 to avoid being killed during the reign of a bloody military dictatorship that lasted until 1982. Her father, my ex-husband, had been jailed by the government. Georgina and I worked with Amnesty International to stop the government officials from killing him.

After a brief stay in Boston, Georgina went to Sweden to be reunited with Ulises (whom we call Mitai, a Guarani word meaning little boy). Sweden accepted them as political refugees, and eventually they became citizens. Initially she worked while he studied to validate his Argentine M.D. She also went to school and completed her doctorate in mathematics. Their first child, Anna, was born in 1979, and a second child, Francisco (Paco), was born two and a half years later.

Odile and I traveled to see Francisco as a newborn, the only hairy black head in a nursery of blond babies! In 1982, Mitaí obtained World Health Organizations funds to go to Nicaragua to organize psychiatric services. Georgina interrupted her career and joined him with their two children. Francisco was only six months old. The war in El Salvador was going on, and I was concerned that the United States might be considering air strikes that would include Nicaragua.

Georgina, Ulises and their family returned to Sweden, and I traveled to visit them a few more times. During one of my visits to Uppsala, I found Georgina too busy to spend time with me, and I decided to take a ferry to Helsinki. I was fascinated by the elegant shops, the local architecture and the art museum, where I appreciated the different natural lighting of the region. I went to get tickets at the stylish opera house but only seats without a stage view were available. I bought one. Once at the theatre, I explained that I had come all the way from Boston to see this opera. They were so impressed that they sat me in the orchestra, in a seat reserved for a guard. The old opera house was charming and the ushers dressed as they had centuries before, with white, elaborate wigs. I heard Oneguin for the first time, sang by a Russian cast. I was delighted! I flew back to the United States, glad to have seen my grandchildren but wondering about my future relationship with them. Happily, my next visits were more satisfying.

Eventually, Georgina became a senior statistician and worked for major corporations with worldwide distribution for the medicines they produced. It was her job to apply mathematics to medicine. Despite the distance, we have a continuous dialogue.

My son Marcelo left home in 1969 when he finished high school. He decided he did not want to attend college, but chose to live on his own for several years. In 1974, he traveled overland from Boston to Argentina. I paid the airfare for his return. Eventually, he, too, got married and had two children. His first child, a daughter, Zucu, was born in Miami in 1982. His second child, Adal, was born in California, two and a half years later. Marcelo and his wife Jano were devotees of a local guru and their devotion to him ruled their lives until they divorced in 1990, the same year that his sister Georgina also got divorced. I visited them both when work and my finances allowed. I was sorry not to see my grandchildren grow, as a grandmother would have liked, but I was thankful for my good fortune at having the two children who were well and far from Argentina where 30,000 of their generation had been killed.

Born a minority in Argentina and having grown up during World War II, I had devoted a great deal of thought and some of my time to social causes. I grew up hearing my father voice his concerns for local and worldwide social and political situations. He instilled a similar concern in me. In Boston in the late sixties, I added my voice to those against the Vietnam War, and even before we met, Florian had been active in the peace movement. The war lasted until the late seventies, and then many of the Vietnamese who had suffered during the bombings, now were suspected of having supported the Americans. Swarms of people escaped in boats and became known as "the boat people."

Our neighboring Episcopalian Church of Dedham offered asylum to one of those families, and living space was provided in a part of the church used to house the nursery school. As soon as the family was settled in, although not a member of the church, I was asked to be their doctor. The request was an indication of how fully the community accepted me as its pediatrician.

The Vietnamese family consisted of parents in their sixties and four children. The oldest daughter had been sent to Italy to study medicine. The second child, a man of about 30, had an easy smile and was perhaps mentally challenged. There were two girls, the youngest of which fit in easily and soon found ways to help others in the community. A younger son, in his late teens, became my patient.

The experience had multiple facets for me. I engaged with these refugees as both their doctor and as a friend. I witnessed their adjustments to their new milieu, and I learned their family dynamics. I learned chiefly from what I saw since their English was limited. I learned that the Vietnamese are given a family name, a middle name and a given name. Dong was their family name. My dealings were always pleasant due to their gentle manners.

As some of the family members found work, their situation improved. The help I offered them decreased with time until one day, the younger daughter Nien came to my home accompanied by her elder sister, a trained pediatrician, who had just arrived from Italy. The sister could speak only Vietnamese or Italian. We communicated in Italian and I began to explain the long process required for her to become certified to practice pediatric medicine in America – the long process I'd gone through years before. Eventually and with great determination, she obtained her degree. The years went by and one day, Dr. Dong appeared in my office, bringing her little girl in as a patient for me to examine and thus completing my circle of service to her family.

Alex's story is also part of my years in Dedham. I lived a short distance from my office, and I even bicycled to work at times. One day I was driving, and a tall, furry dog ran in front of me. I hit the brake but could not avoid hitting the animal. The owner and I rushed to check on the dog's condition. Moments later, the dog stood up and walked. What a relief!

The owner looked familiar. Was she Alex's mother? I had heard that her six-year-old son had been diagnosed with a brain tumor. How terrible it would have been had I hurt the boy's pet! I called that afternoon and confirmed that the dog was fine.

Seven months later, Alex's parents came to my office to ask me to take care of their son. He had completed the radiotherapy and was in remission. He was left with a slight deviation of his gaze and a bit of clumsiness at sports when playing basketball and soccer, but he was getting straight "A"s at Dedham Country Day school.

In the past, things had not been easy for Alex, but he was ready to meet his challenges. A neuropsychological evaluation indicated a superior intelligence and that the boy had high expectations for himself. He was ready to overcome his handicaps and did so with a sense of humor. He had a special charm and serenity beyond his age. He inspired love and respect among his friends and those who cared for him.

Five years later, he collapsed at a basketball game and was taken to the Emergency Room with slurred speech and ataxia – speech difficulty and poor balance. He'd been compensating for the latter by walking with his legs further apart. Back at school, he asked for a single concession: to be given more time to complete his written assignments.

My previous role as the coordinator for a child with subtle chronic problems abruptly changed. In his first admission to The Children's Hospital, a nurse had written on the chart that "…both parents were with him day and night. Many friends visited both the child and his parents." The same comment could have been made for the remainder of Alex's life and I was witness to the attention the family received. Alex became the center of a constellation that attracted each one of us as if we were drawn by a gravitational force. The outpouring of support from children and adults included bringing Alex food, reading to him and even cleaning floors for him.

The disease progressed until on one of my home visits, (it was never clear to me whether it was socially or medically necessary), I discovered that Alex was very ill. His decline occurred after he had received another treatment in a series of radiotherapy. It was hard to determine whether the reason for his severe verbal impairment and quadriparesis was the tumor or to its treatment. He had needed high doses of cortisone, his face was rounder and two of his dorsal vertebras had been fractured, producing pain. I found him propped up in his bed that now occupied the living room. Sitting on a wheel chair was a friend, a girl in the terminal stages of cystic fibrosis, who would precede him in their deadly race. Neither one of them had intelligible speech. But they were entranced in a communication that took place on a level different from the one we know. It was a luminous day, probably around my lunch time, and light seemed to radiate from them. Moved, I felt as if present at a legendary mystic scene.

Alex's schoolmates continued to support him through his downhill slide, displaying unusual clarity in their understanding and adjusting to each new situation. They celebrated a graduation ceremony at his door. Alex died a few weeks later.

On his final ambulance trip to the hospital, his devoted parents were joined by his neurologist (today world famous), a friend of the family, and his pediatrician. When we arrived, someone remarked that they had never seen such a group.

Alex had a graceful way of acknowledging any support given to him. Even in his terminal coma, we saw him blink his eyes when one of his friends held his hand.

I include Alex's story in my own memoir to honor his memory and those of my patients who died. I grieve for each one.

Although medicine occupied my time when I was not at home, my concern for the larger world never abated. In 1973, I joined those who attempted to publicize and stop the brutal political persecutions carried out by the Pinochet government in Chile. In doing so, I became more acquainted with, and joined the Unitarian church in Dedham.

During the winter of 1980, I attended an inspiring meeting at the Unitarian Universalist Service Committee (UUSC) headquarters in Boston, where what we called a Boston Area Unit was born and where I met a remarkable activist named Liz Keil. She was gentle in her manners but persistent in her work which she continued until she died in 2006 at the age of 88. Under the umbrella of the unit, one of several in the country, we searched for those in neighboring Unitarian Universalist (UU) churches who might share a common interest in a particular social issue.

These networks were busy helping the homeless and the refugees from the war in El Salvador, educating the UU members about the United States' role in Central America, and providing support for progressive local candidates.

In 1984, during the Reagan presidency, the Federal Communications Commission relaxed the regulations governing programs with violent themes that were available at hours that children watched TV. Toys and complementary cartoons with violent themes and movies like Rambo began to proliferate. A few months after the regulations were relaxed, my pediatric practice saw an increase in child-to-child injuries. I appealed to my friends in my church's UUSC unit. and we agreed that our children's exposure to violence could not be ignored. This was many years before the shootings at Columbine High School and Sandy Hook Elementary School, and other disasters. We networked with teachers, grandparents, psychologists, and other groups outside our church to address the problem of violence on television. The UUSC preferred to concentrate on other topics and so, striking out on our own, we renamed our group the Boston Area Task Force Against Violent TV and War Toys. These were exciting moments for Liz, Kay and me – meeting people from diverse fields with the same concern about violence, trying to stop the trend. We organized well attended events in Boston and other communities and capitalized on local television opportunities with outlets that would carry our message.

I continued working with this heterogeneous group until I received a grant from the Harvard Community Health Plan (HCHP) Foundation to gather statistics from my anecdotal observations, and to train pediatricians to teach parents about the effect of television on children. The work was exciting and rewarding, but it also added hours to my already busy life. My commitment had grown with my role as the principal investigator and creator of the Violence Prevention Project of the HCHP Foundation. With the aide of advocates I brought on board and the participation of other pediatricians and nurses, we produced and publicized statistics on child-to-child violence and raised awareness about the effects of TV violence. While involved with this project, I also participated in the Massachusetts Medical Society's (MMS) first committee to prevent partner abuse. I designed a few of the first signs that still appear today in medical examining rooms to prevent spousal abuse. Under the auspices of the MMS, we organized a conference on the effects of TV and media violence, long before guns and killings became an issue in American schools.

Only in the late nineties did my activism wane as my physical energy began to decline. At that point I decided that my priority had to be the care of my patients and my financial responsibilities for the care of my parents.

7

Two Deaths: Florian and My Father

I continued to live in denial about Florian's alcohol problem. During a Christmas visit in 1989, Odile and Marcelo confronted me. I had invited Marcelo's children to spend Christmas with us. Marcelo decided to come too. He found Florian in such a condition that he told me quite plainly, "My children are not going in a car driven by Florian." Remarkably, Florian accepted that condition. Odile had brought up Florian's drinking in the past, but I'd always denied it was an issue. This time I was not taken by surprise and I could not ignore the reality any longer. My son and my daughter Odile knew that it was not an easy issue to confront. They sat with me in the cozy library of my house, behind closed doors.

Marcelo told me, "Mom, you have to start going to Al-Anon and you will understand what happened to you." He explained what Al-Anon was. I'd only heard of Alcoholics Anonymous (AA).

Initially, I rejected his suggestion. I couldn't imagine sitting with a group of people I didn't know and discussing the private circumstances of my life. After a few days, however, I realized that I did need help. I searched to find a doctors group of Al-Anon, but it did not exist. I settled for a group in Wellesley where the curtain before my eyes began to lift.

In time, after his family had confronted him repeatedly, Florian finally promised to go for treatment. But Florian approached getting help in his own, unique way. Odile suffered as a result of her father's condition to the extent that she decided that she needed to interrupt her college studies and get him some help. When she did, we were asked to attend family therapy.

Florian would not attend, although I did go. During one session Odile and I were advised that Odile should live apart from her father. By the following Sunday I had arranged to rent a small house where Odile and I could live. Florian, unmoved by our decision, continued drinking. Two months later, Odile moved to New York. I remained in the small house for the following six months. During that period I went with Florian for a single visit to talk to his therapist who I felt was inept. During the session, I demanded that he help Florian with his addiction. As a result, Florian enrolled in a day-program at McLean, a Harvard psychiatric facility. He promised to quit drinking, so I moved back into the Dedham house eight months after leaving it – filled with hope and trusting Florian's promises. Florian did not allow me to attend family therapy, and of course he didn't quit drinking. It was a big disappointment. But at least Odile had, for the time being, escaped being exposed to Florian's alcoholism. She'd taken a job in Manhattan at Dean and De Luca and had an internship with ABC TV in New York.

Over time, I continued to gain insight into Florian's condition. In 1992, as part of my work with the Violence Prevention Project of the Harvard Community Health Plan Foundation and the Committee to Prevent Violence Against Women at the Massachusetts Medical Society, I attended an important conference. Judith Lewis Herman spoke and gave a slide show that drew parallels between battered women and the mistreatment of political prisoners. When she finished, I had to leave the room. I was suffocated by the realization that I was one of those victims. How did I become one? What path had I innocently followed? Was this a slippery slope that we women can fall into? The irony was that I, myself, was instructing professionals on how to recognize domestic violence and on how to protect battered and abused women.

In 1994, I traveled to Argentina, stopping on route in Uruguay to visit my cousin Marcia Stigol and her husband, both psychoanalysts. The trip and spending time with them helped me realize how different and how much better I felt with them and away from my home. It was then that I made the decision to end my marriage.

Once I became aware of what my life was really like and what kind of future I could expect, I made the decision to change my circumstances dramatically. In 1994, I left the beautiful home in Dedham in which I'd lived for 21 years. I moved to a big, empty colonial house in Brookline which was the property of friends who lived nearby, a fortunate circumstance at that moment in my life.

Florian and I were officially divorced in 1995. Even so, this was not to be the end of my relationship with him. We had too many ties and much in common. We were both first generation immigrants. In some ways that bound us, and Florian had little family he could turn to. His remaining family consisted only of a few old survivors from the Nazi Germany era who lived in Argentina and who would be of no help to him.

The strongest bond that tied us was our daughter Odile. During this period, she had returned to school at Vassar and graduated with the class of '95. Florian attended her graduation but he was in bad condition. He stayed for the ceremony itself, but left before the luncheon celebration. Only a friend of Odile and I attended the luncheon. I knew I would have to continue to try to help Florian. If I did not, Odile would have to carry that burden. I could not allow that. It was clear our issues with Florian were not over.

Odile moved to Atlanta and while visiting her, I learned how much worse Florian's alcoholism had become and how tied Odile was to her father's issue. We had just returned to Odile's apartment from a nearby coffee shop when we heard the following message from Florian on her answering machine. "I was brought to Faulkner Hospital emergency room and they are keeping me here," said her father's voice.

I returned to Boston on the first available flight and went straight to the hospital. There I found Florian in the D. T. (detoxification) unit, deeply sedated, with his wrists and legs tied to his bed. In his delirium, he had grabbed a piece of metal and attempted to hit one of the nurses. His cleaning lady, who had faithfully worked for us for years, had found him unconscious on the kitchen floor of the big Dedham house. He was covered with bruises, had fallen downstairs at night, and had managed to drag himself to the kitchen near the bottom of the stairs. He had fallen in a stupor and was not able to call anyone. She called 911.

After a week of delirium tremens in the D.T. Unit, Florian's survival was questionable. I had to call Odile, who flew in from Atlanta. Later, when he finally recovered, he was to speak about the pain of seeing his anguished daughter sitting next to him, which he said prompted his determination to stop drinking.

Did he ever really stop? Even now I am never sure. After his stay at Faulkner, he was sent to the Spaulding Rehabilitation Center in Boston.

I visited him there a day after his admission. He told me, "They don't know what they are doing here." He looked like a shadow – the skin on his face sagging and his eyes sunken. The next day, he signed himself out and returned home with no food or anyone to care for him. I had an important office party to attend and decided to drop a few cans of food off for him on my way. A few months later he seemed to be sober, and he invited our daughter and me to accompany him on a cruise. It was 1998. Florian had inherited money after our divorce and was eager to spend it. By then I was completely detached from him, thanks in some part to Al-Anon. I agreed to join him on the cruise, knowing it would be easier for Odile if I came. We went to Istanbul and Greece. He had a cabin for himself and one for Odile and me. No alcohol was consumed and the trip was pleasurable and without rancor. A few months later Florian invited us again to Sicily. Our tour stopped for three days in beautiful Taormina. While Odile and I went for a walk, a friend of hers reported that he had seen Florian drinking. Our hopes for his lasting recovery from alcoholism vanished, even as his needs for daily care grew.

Florian continued living in the Dedham house, with the help of various caregivers. When we divorced, he gave me money corresponding to half the value of the house, money I did not know he had. After my stay in Brookline, I had rented a one bedroom apartment in Newton. During a busy day at my office in June of 2000, my nurse timidly handed me a newspaper clipping. In a low voice, she said, "Did you know about this?" The front page of the local newspaper told a sad story in detail. My ex-husband, having relapsed after two years of sobriety, was driving under the influence and hit his neighbor. The journalist described extensive leg injuries to the victim and the fogged state of mind of the driver. I was angry. Here was Florian, the man who had destroyed our family life, who had obliged me to abandon my home and who deeply affected my daughter, and now once more he was acting irresponsibly. The circumstances of the accident were harrowing. His neighbor had been standing behind an ambulance that was about to transport his sick child. I thought of my own patients and about the possibility that one day Florian could smash his car into them. Distressed, I later went to talk to the police chief whom I knew well. I begged him to take Florian's license, which of course, he had no authority to do. Until a judge could stop him, Florian was free to drive legally in Massachusetts.

When I finished reading the article and had a free moment in my workday, I called Florian. He was lucid enough to be afraid. He asked me to be present at the next meeting with his lawyer. There, I learned that, unknown to me or Odile, there had been a previous first offense. Florian had hit the central rail of the Massachusetts turnpike a few months before. Fortunately no one was hurt.

Pondering the recent accident, I felt sorrow. A man had been badly hurt. Florian had followed the inexorable destiny of an alcoholic. And I felt bad for myself too. Here I was, still involved in a nightmare I'd been trying to escape for ten years. I considered the situation from the point of view of my profession. As a physician, I accepted the fact that Florian was a sick man who needed treatment. Being a doctor, I was able to get him a bed at the psychiatric hospital of Harvard Medical School, the pride of Boston. I called to tell him what I had done, despite the great difficulty of finding such a bed. Florian refused to go. I told him firmly, "Florian, you go now to McLean's or you will not see me again."

When he heard my threat, he yielded. On the evening of July 3, I drove him to the hospital. Leaving the somber corridors of the admission unit, I felt exhausted. I also knew that I had done something good – both for Florian and for society.

I had to stay at his home, now also my responsibility, and I had to care for his dog, a Doberman, whom I feared. "Why am I sleeping back in Dedham?" I asked myself after I left Florian in the hospital that night. "Why?" I felt that I could not abandon him in his disgraceful circumstances. I had wanted him admitted to a hospital for detoxification as soon as possible: for three reasons. First, he needed to stop driving in his present condition and clear his mind. Secondly, the idea that unless hospitalized Florian might have to go to jail, broke my heart. Third, I reasoned that if he took steps to deal with his alcoholism, a judge might be more lenient about sending him to jail. My stay in Dedham would end when he left the hospital. I did not want to focus on the fact that I was back in my beloved old home. Doing so would have caused a turmoil of feelings that I could not afford at the moment. It had taken me a long time to find peace in a home away from the Dedham house. In addition, I had to face Odile's wrath. I had tried to protect her and lighten her burden by putting Florian in a hospital, but she was upset that he was placed there against his will.

I celebrated the 4th of July holiday of 2000 taking care of Florian's house, his dog, and by visiting Florian in the psychiatric ward, a considerable distance away. The environment in which he was sequestered was a sad one: an old building with a majestic front and a poorly designed interior that was dark and dirty, with old rugged furniture, decaying floors and the usual, forlorn characters one would expect. I found him in shock and hardly talking. Four days later, the case worker assigned to him said he was in such a poor state that guardianship would be necessary. An important meeting was scheduled for the following Monday morning with the psychiatrist in charge of his case. At that time we were to hear the complete evaluation of his condition. I canceled work to attend, even though Monday morning was the busiest morning of my practice.

The meeting was a fiasco. I was told Florian needed long-term care and months in a rehabilitation institute. Yet two days later they sent him home, alone by taxi, with no explanation for the apparent change in diagnosis and no chance to discuss the matter with the doctors. Odile arrived from New York where she was living, still working for CNN. She let me know that she did not trust the lawyer her father had hired to defend him from the car accident. Fortunately, Odile changed her mind after she met the lawyer – one less reason for me to be troubled.

So there I was once again, accompanying Florian to meetings with his lawyer. Despite my current presence in his life, our relationship was vastly different. How much time, after all, had gone by since we had really functioned as man and woman, as husband and wife? As a woman with a history of having been emotionally abused by an alcoholic husband, I certainly did not owe him anything. Through all the years that we had been separated, I had given him whatever moral support I could. He was financially independent and could keep the house. And my own independence after our divorce could not be disputed. Yet Florian saw my return to his home not as a transitory measure but as a permanent move back. In spite of our separation and divorce, he was only able to think of me still as his dutiful wife. We needed to have a session with his current counselor at the Faulkner Hospital addiction unit where he was now treated under a court mandate. I hoped that that alone would make him realize that things had changed.

The day after that meeting, we went to see a movie called "*Sunshine*," the painful saga of a Hungarian-Jewish family. The movie had a special significance for me, since Florian was also a victim of the Holocaust. Knowing as much as I did about his past, and knowing the heartbreak of his own family's diaspora, I felt that I could not abandon him. But at the same time, I had to try my best and come out of this intact. Was it even possible?

My two-days stay again in Dedham included accompanying Florian to two court appearances. The first took place at the Brighton court where he admitted to the first drunk-driving accident, the one without victims.

In his second appearance, thanks to the kindness of his victim and his judge, Florian was ordered to two weeks at a DUIL (driving under the influence of liquor) program. In both instances there was somebody I knew in the court who, alarmed, came to ask how they could assist me. I had a chance to appreciate how wise I had been to divorce him and not to have continued in the role of codependent wife.

I drove Florian to attend the DUIL program which was an hour and a half from Boston, and I picked him up. He needed my help in the admission process when they asked him routine questions. Rich and poor, black and white, men and women – the people with him in the program were all being treated for a second offense of uncontested drunk driving. And yet the personnel there treated everyone with consideration and courtesy. I respected that, but in some ways it also disgusted me – to see individuals treated courteously in spite of behavior which endangered the lives of others.

Finally, after a week, I found a friend of mine who would stay with Florian in the house, and I was spared a second disquieting sojourn. Then shortly after his return from the DUIL program, we found a second kind soul, one who needed a salary, to care for him four days a week. That left me free to escape to New York and have fun with my two extraordinary daughters – independent and capable women – Odile working for CNN and Georgina, visiting from Sweden, still a capable statistician working for a prominent international pharmaceutical company. Odile and Georgina made me feel that I had accomplished my role in this world.

A brief trip to New Jersey allowed me to see my dear cousin, Carlitos, still looking well before succumbing to cancer. Soon I left for one week in Argentina where I visited my father and step-mother and I saw other family members and friends. I gave a series of lectures on violence and television. I was able to get Florian out of my mind for a while.

At the end of October 2000, the same day that Florian appeared in court for a second time, my cousin, Carlitos, died. When his son tried to reach me in the middle of the night, I was at Florian's home, supporting him emotionally in the aftermath of his recent trial. At the request of his victim, he was not jailed but merely ordered to continue with the traditional rehabilitation programs mandated by law, including visits to counselors, AA meetings, and to two psychiatrists. I went with him to Atlanta to visit our daughter for Christmas. There, in the hotel bar, he drank nonstop. Why and for how long do my daughter and I have to endure this, I asked myself. On the flight back to Boston, the smell of alcohol on his breath was unbearable. A piece of paper fell from his pocket. I opened it. It was a receipt for two vodkas that he had paid for with cash. Why bother with all those programs and all the pretense of rehabilitation, I wondered? Why not let him do as he wants – just as we give cancer patients the choice of whether to be treated or not? The day after our return was his birthday. To celebrate what?

Meantime, my aging father was ailing. Aside from his blindness, he was aware of his many other limitations. During my last trip to visit him in Argentina, I had organized his 95th birthday party. We did not talk that much; we merely held hands. I observed how he would take a series of deep breaths. He was probably aware of his weakening heart. He had decided "no more hospital visits or procedures," during what became the last six months of his life.

Even after I returned home, I could tell by his voice during our frequent phone conversations that he was ailing. He was very short of breath. He kept trying to hide it from me and refused any intervention until finally, when he agreed to go to the hospital to die. I called him later in the day and he told me that he was perfect – with his usual inexhaustible optimism.

In Buenos Aries, Theo Sadler had been my father's doctor; and after him, his son Alberto took care of him devotedly. Even so, my father's health kept going downhill. He seemed very conscious of his deteriorating condition and did not seem to want to take Herculean efforts to change it.

Since his 95th birthday that March, I realized his mind was not the same, and instead of sustaining a long conversation with me, he would greet me in his usual loving way and quickly hand the telephone to Esther. I knew that soon I would not hear any more "Mi Luisita..." when he answered the phone.

Even then, I could not conceive of life without him. The very thought of it caused my chest to constrict and for sobs to well up from the deepest part of my soul. I tried hard to be rational and carry on with my life, thinking of how lucky I was to have such a beautiful relationship with him. It had been uninterrupted, with love and devotion flowing both ways to cover emotional and material needs. It was the essential and unique privilege that I had in my life. His wisdom gave me the values I live by; his love gave me the energy to be able to provide love to others; his material support to my older children and myself was the basis of the comforts we enjoy today

On June 14, 2001, my father died. He was 95. Despite the tragedy of my mother's death, he had managed to live the rest of his life with a smile, thanks in part to his utterly kind disposition, his intelligence, his good sense, and the love of my stepmother. Despite some cultural differences, I always got along with my father's second wife, Esther, and her family. My stepmother was fully dedicated to my father as he was to her. She was fully a part of his life; in fact, once they were married, I could never really talk with my father alone or write a letter to him only. But he was very happy with Esther with whom he had been married for 49 years. She in turn was generous to me, my children, and also to my brother.

When I moved from Dedham to Brookline in 1994, my new home was near the First Parish Church. During the previous years I had worked as a volunteer for the Unitarian Universalist Service Committee (UUSC), and found that congregation to my liking. (They had deep interests in some of the world issues that I had.) Their pastor had a strong personality and a privileged intellect. I have attended meetings on the prevention of violence in that church since 1997. I found the sermons by the pastor, David Johnson, provocative, reflecting on the same concerns I had frequently considered, but had too little time to explore. At the warm invitation of his wife, I spent many holidays at his family table. In June of 2001 when my father died, only the Pastor knew about my father's death and perhaps considered it a normal passage of life. Nobody from my church approached me. I had no family in Boston, and it was a lonely mourning except for calls and e-mails from distant places and the sympathy and understanding of the personnel working with me.

My mourning period for my father was long and intense. I continued to think about what he meant to me. He lived to 95 because he was determined to live. First, he did not want to leave his wife Esther alone. He knew how much she depended on him. In 1993, her niece Rachel had died of cancer at 27. Esther and my father had raised Rachel since she was five years old. My stepmother never recovered from that loss, which also greatly pained my father.

There is no aspect of my life that hasn't been influenced by my father's teachings, comments, his tastes, and the examples he set for me. My father lived surrounded by the affection he had earned. He taught us to live in harmony with others. "Seek equanimity," he used to repeat, meaning that we should find the spiritual and physical balance that he himself tried to live with. Two weeks following his death, I wrote, "The transition between having him and not having him occurs in a bath of peace and love."

I had business to do concerning his death. A few years earlier, in a moving dialogue of limited words, he had let me know that he wanted me to be in charge of his wife. Esther died about three years after my father in May 2004. She was very well cared for until her heart gave up.

My father's memory and love will remain with me for as long as I live and will endure on these pages afterward. A journalist who knew my father from the years he spent with Esther at his beloved "quinta," described meeting him on a warm night, on March 11 of 1977. He wrote his observations in *Reflections: A Doctor at the Gate by Ismael Garzon:*

> It was the celebration of his birthday and many people, his friends from the town of "Capilla del Senior "(Chapel of the Lord), were there.
>
> A colleague, Lionel Godoy, introduced me to him. Godoy knew him and had shared his friendship for a long time.
>
> From that moment on, a link of spiritual identity, an idiosyncrasy, he would call it with irony, was established between the two of us.
>
> As we walked through his park, he spoke to me about Victor Hugo, Michelangelo, Petorutti, Soldi, Borges, Hernandez, Guiraldes and any ghost of the world of poetry, plastic arts and literature one can imagine. He spoke slowly, in a colloquial and kind manner, without any hint of an assuming erudition. 'Fall is the best season of the year. We recreate our romantic inspiration, matching the golden color of the falling leaves' ... 'Walk slowly,' he said, 'let your anxieties be discharged in the earth under your feet and look at the stars'; and referring to "Martin Fierro," that the stars; 'seem even more beautiful when we feel more in disgrace and as if God had created them for our consolation.

His usual attire was the typical gaucho's baggie pants and boots. An elegant thick ornamented belt, a kerchief at the neck and an eternal smile on his face. Doctor Stigol (and here I remember Alberto Gerchunoff) opened for me the doors of his house and of his heart. I found many times a fraternal refuge in his timely and wise advice.

In the world of my dreams and memories, he will remain as one of the unforgettable characters in my life. The "doctor at the gate," as he is known by neighbors who approached him for advice or they go to him for questions about their physical or emotional health.

He left his bucolic surroundings with some melancholy. He returned to a city habitat, in the heart of it, Corrientes and Montevideo. He joined the eternal night of Buenos Aires. He continues now in his splendid eighty-six years, always in love and courting eternally his beloved wife Ester.

My father gone, I had to continue to deal with a different kind of sorrow; the tragedy of Florian as the drama continued. Odile tried to help him and to make sense of Florian's assets and his expenses. Her close involvement led to a constant friction between them since, although Florian continued attending rehabilitation meetings, he also kept drinking. His mind was constantly floating in a deeply dysfunctional state. He was often rude and aggressive to our daughter and to me and getting worse as time progressed. His belly swelled due to the compensatory hypertrophy of his cirrhotic liver. He was lonely and confused. Odile was often upset at him for not taking care of himself. I could see her challenging role as his daughter needed to be resolved. I was also hurt as a witness to all of this. I was often a referee between them and could not see any way out. I attended Al-Anon intermittently when I felt that the burden of Florian was too heavy. It was not fair to dedicate all my life to it. Seeing him so sick and seeing him alone, struggling against the monster of his addiction that had reached the intimacy of his cellular structure, continued to produce a surge of pity in me. Florian was the slave of his craving, and we could not judge him as we could a free man. But his slow destruction affected my daughter – and me. My headaches and my insomnia, my muscle pains, and the tightness in my chest were the product of his constant intrusion into my life.

About eight months before his death early in 2004, it became clear that his derangement was affecting me to such a degree that I might die before he did. Frightened at that thought, I realized that the time had come to ask my daughter to take over his care. He had become a burden that made me ill and weakened me, and I had to carry the responsibility of my big pediatric practice and my need to earn money to support myself and my parents. I was seventy-three when Odile took over the care of her father and became his legal guardian. Years later I would regret my request, given the impact this yoke had on her.

As Florian continued to deteriorate, he became too incapacitated to live alone, and I hired a young man who turned out to be helpful and honest. A year and a half before his death, I stopped one morning at his home to leave my car parked there for a few hours. A friend was to meet me and drive to Williamstown on a day that was beautiful and sunny. I went briefly inside to say hello. The young man who was then living in the house informed me that Florian was in bed and not feeling well. I found him indeed dehydrated and confused, as if his end were near. Would it have been better to let his downhill state continue? But I could not do it. I called an ambulance, and he was transported once more to Faulkner hospital. Since a previous fall downstairs had prevented me from leaving for a trip to New York, this time I did not rush to the emergency room. When I arrived a couple of hours later, I found him very agitated. The medical resident who saw his liver had told him that a transplant was needed. After this episode and back at home, Florian was aggressive with the young man who cared for him at his home. He also attacked a night nurse with his cane. A year before, my daughter Odile had removed him from an Alzheimer unit where he stayed while I was in Europe. This time she recognized that there was no other alternative other than to have Florian institutionalized. I had lived the last years watching him deteriorate as if in a *"Portrait of Dorian Grey"* – a terrible sight, but when I went with him to a hospital, I would be reminded that I had no legal authority to help him since we were divorced.

My daughter and I looked at several places, and we found Spring House, a non-profit institution located across the street from Faulkner Hospital. The newly assigned young doctor reviewed Florian's medical history, looked at the list of his visits to the emergency room, and decided that his condition required hospice services. Odile paid for two nurses to provide twenty-four hour coverage, and she supplemented Spring House's regular staff until Florian's death on February 7, 2004.

Up to his death, in Florian's mind, I was still his wife. He expected my daily visits. I recall that if I missed a day, he'd shout, "Where is my wife?"

I recollect one visit when I could understand him despite his tendency now to merely mumble. When he saw me, he asked, "Did you bring my socks?" Two days before he had given me a pair of his socks to mend because it is the duty of a good wife to mend the husband's socks.

"Yes," I answered.

"Put them on," he said.

I did and after a while, as if in a delirium, he asked me, "Can I come live in your apartment?"

I answered, "My apartment is really small. Do you remember? It has only one bedroom."

"Maybe we can find another apartment in the same building," he answered.

"You have your house," I said.

"I never go there," he said. "I know I will not be able to return but I don't want my books to disappear. I am a prisoner here. I don't have any money even to take a cab. Women always find a way to take control of things."

"Florian," I said, "you are a prisoner of your illness. I don't control anything."

These conversations alternated between his delirious thoughts and his orders – given in aggressive tones.

In December he appeared semi-comatose, unable to communicate with the Hospice volunteer or with me. We didn't know if he could hear us. He responded to his caretaker for essential needs. One of his arms twitched uncontrollably. He tried to get up and did not succeed. The caretaker helped him to lie back down. He mumbled an apology. The next day Florian would be 72 years old.

The Hospice volunteer thought that, at one point, Florian wanted to speak to a rabbi, which wasn't characteristic. Previously Florian had kicked out a pastor who had gone to visit him and had told me, "I don't want any of those…"

When Florian died, Odile organized the funeral service at the church I attended – the First Parish in Brookline. A pianist played Mozart and some of Florian's friends attended. One of his friends who spoke said, "Florian's enemies were war and racism."

Three Vietnamese teenagers who had suffered poliomyelitis were there with prostheses that Florian had paid for in his last years. Florian wasn't a bad man; he was a sick man. Alcohol had destroyed him and taken its toll on his family.

In the same year that Florian died, 2004, I was diagnosed with ovarian cancer.

8

Cancer

Still recovering from the ordeal of Florian's death, in August of 2004, I was diagnosed with ovarian cancer. I'd been overdue for an appointment with my gynecologist, but I had so little energy left after caring for Florian that I postponed it. I knew that HMO's recommend that women my age need a Pap smear only every two years. With that in mind, I wasn't especially concerned when I delayed the routine checkup.

The year before, while caring for Florian, I'd noticed that my belly and waist seemed enlarged, changes which I had mentioned to my doctor. She ordered an abdominal ultrasound but not a pelvic ultrasound and found nothing wrong. Frequent urination with normal urine should have flagged the possibility of ovarian cancer. But I was a pediatrician with little experience concerning those signs.

The physiatrist in our group, having expertise only in muscle related problems, prescribed the latest analgesic when my leg pains continued. The next complaint to my clinician produced a prescription for antidepressants but no further physical exams were ordered after two nonspecific blood tests came back clear. I did not take the antidepressants. Still, I was haunted by the sense that something wasn't right. I was used to working long hours, yet I felt exhausted when I saw the list of patients still left to be seen when three o'clock rolled around at my office. I attributed my reaction to old age.

I had planned two weekend visits that summer: one to Washington and one to see an exhibition in Tennessee. I canceled both at the last minute. I had no energy for either trip. Instead, I went to see Odile in New York. We needed to be together to support each other. I slept with her and her cat. That's when it became clear to me that something was terribly wrong. I could no longer deny it.

In bed that night, Odile's cat walked on my belly and I awoke screaming in pain. The next morning I examined my abdomen and noticed something hard that was not supposed to be there. Back in Boston, although I suspected something serious, again I delayed a visit to my gynecologist for a few days.

When I finally contacted him and told him what I'd felt, I got an appointment in two days. He examined me, and, unable to hide his upset, he told me that I had an ovarian tumor and that at my age they were usually malignant. The tumor was big enough to push the uterus up and this was the hard organ that I'd felt. My first thought when he ordered the ultrasound was that it was nine in the morning. I had more than twenty of my own patients scheduled for that day. The ultrasound Dr. Goldstein ordered was done the next day and it confirmed his suspicions.

The only good news, if there was any to be had, was that the tumor's protuberance thankfully led to an early diagnosis which seldom occurs with that kind of treacherous cancer.

I had faced many difficult challenges in my life, and I had always had the emotional energy to cope with them. I thought I would be able to manage this one too, like all the others. But this was different. Was Dr. Goldstein's diagnosis a death sentence? Numb after receiving the news, I climbed into my car. I was unable to recognize the streets and the same roads that I'd driven for the last thirty years between that hospital and my office. I was driving but I didn't know where I was going.

I hesitated to worry Odile with the news, but I had no choice but to let her know as I was going to undergo major surgery with an uncertain outcome. Odile was the only one of my children present to learn the news at that time. D.P. Goldstein, my gynecologist operated without delay. My grand-daughter Zucu happened to be in Boston at the time. Alex Sadler and his friend sat with Odile awaiting news of the surgery with hope and dread.

I was familiar with the hospital since I had worked there for 31 years, and I had total confidence in my surgeon who I know had out-of-the-ordinary skills. A sense of serenity came over me as they wheeled me on a gurney towards the operating room.

When I blinked my eyes and awoke slowly after the operation, Dr. Goldstein came to me and gave me hope. He said the operation had been successful, and that it was his belief they'd successfully removed the tumor.

But back home a week later, I received a call from Dr. Goldstein. It remains a vivid moment in my memory. He was calling to tell me that the tumor had been removed. But the cancer cells that may have spilled in my abdomen during the surgery were the most aggressive kind. Chemotherapy was mandatory.

I recalled the difficulties my cousin had with cancer and her chemotherapy treatments. In 1966, I had been the caretaker for her when she came to Boston from Argentina to battle cancer. Dr. Goldstein had also been her doctor. I witnessed her struggle during her chemotherapy treatments which required hospitalization. I also recalled the secondary effects that chemotherapy had on a dear friend and additionally on the mother of one of my patients. I was terrified at the thought that I would suffer as they did, and I told Odile that I would refuse chemotherapy. It was difficult enough that in the process of recovering from the surgery, I had to walk with a cane. During the thorough search of my lymph nodes during my surgery, a nerve going to my right leg had been cut.

As the summer of 2004 ended, I recuperated. Through the large windows of my bedroom, the trees and the blue sky were inviting. I longed to go outside, and when I did, taking step after difficult step, each day I was able to extend the length of my path. A month later, I was able to walk without a cane, but I still had to face the coming consult with the oncologist. I can remember my visit to her: the room, the corridors, the bright light of the sun that filtered through the windows, and my fears. Odile had been told that the chemotherapy treatments offered hope, and she urged me to reconsider. She accompanied me in the waiting room, and entered the doctor's office with me. I was prepared to give my reasons for not having chemotherapy. To my surprise, when I left an hour and a half later, I had agreed to the treatments. Dr. Matulonis's last words, "We are going to beat this cancer," still resonate in my ears, and her friendly face is always with me. The vision of her encouraging me still brings me to tears. We human beings do help one another sometimes and in such profound ways.

My daughter Odile cried when she learned I would go ahead with treatments that could mean my survival. Odile continued in her role as my caretaker. Odile and I braved my chemos with intermittent calls from distant friends and family. We cherished the few who tried to remain closer to us. I felt so sick at times that I did not know whether it was better to receive a call or not. I needed the calls badly, but I often had no energy to talk when I did get them. The Dana-Farber Cancer Institute suggested activities to help patients deal with their diagnosis and recovery. I chose one of them: writing. I knew the comforting effect writing can provide, and I decided to continue to write my memoir, urged to do so by David, a volunteer, who took the time to encourage me.

I knew that chemotherapy can disrupt the body's functions, and that it is hard to deal with. But my most serious uncertainty was how my brain would be affected. Even though I was seventy-four, I was still a full time pediatrician. I was a member of the Advisory Committee of the Radcliffe Mentor Program. I could go to New York and enjoy my subscription to the Metropolitan Opera, and I enjoyed the art world in Boston too. What would be left of my intellectual abilities and of my ego? Would I still be able to live a rich life?

I worried about my patients. It felt like an insurmountable wall had been erected between my patients of more than thirty years and myself. My illness had isolated me from my work. I had deserted my patients without explanations or farewells. Servicing them had been the center of my life, and I was failing them. I myself had become the needy patient. I cried every time I thought of it, and I still find it difficult to talk about. I still dream repeatedly of going back to take care of them, even nine years after my retirement. The cards I received from many of my beloved and loyal patients lifted my spirits enormously, and were our only remaining contact.

I received my first chemotherapy treatment in September of 2004. It took me a few days until I could sit and a few more to walk again. Odile's loving care lifted me back on my feet. A massage therapist raised my spirit and restored some life to my weakened muscles. Eight days after the treatment, I was able to sit at the computer and write.

One of the cancer survivors I met, Karen, suggested I attend a group meeting at the Beth Israel Hospital. It was run by an experienced social worker, Hester Hill. So two weeks after my first treatment, still disoriented, I went to my first session seeking support. The group included a mixture of women in different stages of their fight with cancer. Some had recently been diagnosed, some faced recurrences, some were survivors and free of disease. All were educated and capable of intelligent discussions. The meeting proved a deep but necessary experience for me. We were sisters bonded by the uncertainty with which we all lived. They helped me as I shared their agony. The loss of one of our group was the hardest part of it: saying goodbye to Michele; later to Debora and later even to the brilliant Karen, a video artist. I could not escape the fact that now I was nothing more than a cancer patient, unable to work, fighting my disease, and fighting for my life.

It broke my heart to learn that one of my patients since his birth, now a medical student at Tufts University, wanted to do his Pediatric rotation with me, and I could not be available for him. I remember discussing career options with him when he was just a young student.

Illness imposes unwanted interludes in our lives. Some of us despair. Some of us are intent in finding ways to avoid being shattered. During the long hours I spent sitting on a sofa or lying on my bed, I did not feel alone when daydreaming about my patients – those whose written words had reached me. For example, I consoled myself by remembering Lane, a fountain of love to her family but whose life was filled with so many difficulties. She was a wonderful character and well worth knowing. I'd met her when her older son was a baby who screamed non-stop. I became concerned and ordered a series of tests to find a reason for his screaming. I don't remember if or how I found a solution, but the mother had been my faithful patient for the last twenty-six years. Lane was petite, with a fragile appearance. Her yellow dyed, long bangs almost covered her forehead. She worked nights, and during the day she took care of her children and then her grandchildren. I can't imagine when she slept. Lane had three daughters and I'd taken care of them as well. As the years passed, I became a witness to the family's struggles.

While I was recovering, Lane's first son, already an adult, died in a motorbike accident, and there I was, unable to provide support. All that I could do was to take care of myself and hope I would get back on my feet one day.

Odile saved me. Writing helped too. After my first chemotherapy treatment, I wrote the following in my diary:

"Today is exactly three weeks after my first chemo. It was supposed to be the date of my second one but it needed to be postponed because of a bout of severe constipation and I had an anal fissure. Today I could relieve myself after three hellish days. I couldn't help but compare what I went through with the unavoidable pain suffered by a prisoner being tortured.

Now, a bit better, my spirit was lifted by Mozart's music and one of my patient's cards helped me smile again."

During my illness, writing helped me in several ways. First, it gave me something enjoyable to do with my time and second, it allowed me to release difficult emotions.

Another segment I wrote in my diary was, fittingly, about hair:

> Odile's cat Mishi is a loving pet that needs human contact, day and night. But his hair ends up on my clothes, the sofa where I sit and even sometimes, on the dining room table. There was no escape from it despite my carefully planned maneuvers. I would dress where the cat didn't go. I even wore special clothes inside the apartment, then changed before going out. A convenient roller with adhesive paper is an important part of my daily routine when I visit my daughter in New York.

> While Mishi's hair had been the problem, now, after the chemo, my own hair has become the issue. This last month I found hair all over my own apartment and this time I was the culprit, not Mishi. Since I was told that I would lose my hair due to the chemotherapy, I decided to cut it shorter. My hairdresser left me with a punk, new look, but it did not last very long. My hair is now as ubiquitous as Mishi's despite all my efforts. As all women do, I always complained about my hair, which was straight and without any gracious waves. I only began to like my new look when I began to lose my precious hair. In a few days, none will be left.

> Even though a wig is available that's a fine replica of my last hairdo, I prefer hats. Besides, they give me an excuse to visit the diverse millinery shows of Boston and New York.

The loss of my hair was not all that was happening to me as a result of the drugs I was given. Taxol had secondary effects, and these included shooting pains. They hit my hands and legs the hardest. I was weak, too dizzy to get up and in too much pain to read or think about anything other than how to find a position that hurt the least.

During my chemotherapy, I was taken care of by a team of the most dedicated and efficient nurses. But the slightest annoyance during my care was enough to trigger deep and disproportionate anger. It was part of my condition. I was on constant guard, living in a state of alert to any additional injury. I monitored every aspect of my care including my diet. During one of my treatments a dietitian came to give her advice and gave me a list of things to eat. Beets were highly recommended, so I had a Russian woman come once a week to prepare a borscht for me. I'm sure this delicious soup contributed to my healing.

But the chemo treatments continued relentlessly. Eighteen days after my third treatment, I still found it hard to sit or stand. I reached a point when I had no interest in reading or listening to music. I lay in bed staring at the top of my wardrobe. I had ordered a box of books before the chemo began with the hope that I would read during my sick days. It lay unopened. The small radio that brought me the classical music that had been my spiritual refuge now ceased to sing.

Malaise had never afflicted me in a manner that produced this kind of inaction.

"When is it going to end?" I often wondered. "Perhaps the best outcome would be an end to 'everything,'" I sometimes thought that death would be a liberation.

In the meantime, Odile was in her father's house in Dedham, organizing his possessions, selecting which of her father's belongings she should keep, and searching meticulously for clues about his life. I managed to go with her a couple of times, hoping to help. My own pain was diluted by the immensity of hers. She worked under pressure, trying to meet a deadline to release the house to the new owners. It had been my own house for more than twenty years, and the sadness was a painful distraction to the pain I felt about my medical condition. In what way, I sometimes wondered, was my ovarian cancer, the melanoma of my brother and the pancreatic cancer of my mother related? Later research would confirm that there was a genetic relationship.

While receiving my chemotherapy, I was given the option of attending relaxation exercises. I had never done them before, but I decided to go. It took place in a large room in an annex of the Dana Farber Cancer. The carpeting that covered the floor featured an outline of the same labyrinth found at the floor of the Chartres Cathedral in France. Initially, I did not understand why it was it appeared at Dana Farber and knew only of the Minotaur labyrinth. When I hesitantly began to walk and follow its path, I found myself concentrating on it and I forgot my anxieties. Weak as I was, I began to dream of returning to Chartres. The experience of taking that walk during my illness was profound, and it was as if a prayer had been answered when three years later I found myself walking on the old stone labyrinth at Chartres.

Finally I had my fourth and last chemotherapy treatment. Fourteen days later I had my most active day up to that point. I attended a church service, saw a movie and had dinner at a friends' house. Everybody commented on how well I looked.

I'd worked hard to look good. I followed a careful diet. I went for a variety of therapies that promised to help, as long as their various approaches seemed rational. They included learning about makeup, eye and brow liners, and for the first time in my life I bought the necessary tools to hide the effects of the chemotherapy treatments on my face. A final touch was the elegant hats I bought that spared me the use of a wig, although my hair had thinned and my scalp felt like it was burning. (I had only four chemotherapy treatments instead of the usual six after I read a report that said that four rather than the traditional six treatments were recommended for patients in my condition. After consulting my doctors, we were all in agreement.)

In early December of that dreadful year, I felt so weak that I requested a blood test. The results confirmed that my white count was very low. I was advised to stay home and avoid contact that might expose me to infection. I received this advice at a time when I'd been considering a return to my pediatric practice. Needless to say the news came as a disappointment, coming at a time when I'd been feeling considerable anxiety about my future career. I began to realize that I might not be able to return to my profession, and I began to consider other possibilities that might fulfill my need for a goal in my life. I needed one to provide me with the energy to survive.

I'd had an interview with the Unitarian Universalist Service Committee, where I'd done volunteer work, to explore the possibility of working for them. I thought that doing so could add meaning to my efforts to survive. But I was denied the opportunity. All I could do was to read alone and wait for the time to come when I'd be allowed to go out and resume my routine.

Winters had always been difficult for me. I used to count the days until spring. The threat of snow on the ground was like a Damocles sword that hung over me because I would have to drive to my office or the hospital regardless of road conditions. I did it for forty years as I had patients who needed me. This winter, however, my surgery provided an excuse to refuse driving in bad weather. Instead, I rejoiced and looked at the white beautiful landscape through my windows.

Slowly, life improved. I was permitted to see others again, and my social life improved. I had moments when it seemed that it might not be so awful to enjoy life without having to go to work every day. A kind of emotional "amnesia" about my diagnosis set in, allowing me to live my days, encouraged by the doctors' hopes that I could be cured.

I continued to recuperate, and before long it was December 31, Florian's birthday, ten months following his death. The date came as it had every year of course. Yet reminiscing about his death, I felt like the world was filled with tragedy. I also felt the deaths of several patients as a personal loss. One of them, Susan, died after she turned fifty. I'd met her when she was in her early teens. She had been paralyzed by a tumor in her spine. When we met, she could still sit, but as her tumor progressed she had to live in an iron lung. Despite that limitation she learned Greek to the point that she could read the Scriptures in Greek. She helped and communicated with everybody around her and even allowed my ex-colleagues from the Department of Physiology at the Harvard School of Public Health to do research on her. One of them gave me a ride so I could be present at her memorial service.

As December progressed, I decided to try to put my grief behind me and to start the New Year resolving to regain the joy and achievements of my previous years. I was determined to recover my life.

A poem called "*This Cruel Age Has Deflected Me*," by Anna Akhmatova, a Russian poet, from a book given to me by a neighbor, resonated with me.

I know beginnings, I know endings too,
And life-in-death, and something else
I'd rather not recall just now.
And a certain woman has usurped my place
and bears my rightful name,
leaving a nickname for my use,
with which I've done the best I could.
The grave I go to will not be my own.
But if I could step outside myself
and contemplate the person that I am,
I should know at last what envy is.

9

Post Cancer, 2005

The "year of my cancer," 2004, finally ended. I was excited each time I was able to return to another of the activities I had stopped due to my surgery and my chemos. When Georgina had come to visit me for Christmas 2004, in my debilitated condition I'd felt as if I were the toddler and she was the mother. That was beginning to change as I grew stronger. Following the New Year, I visited New York and enjoyed the company of Odile and my granddaughter Anna, Georgina's child – and even of Mishi the cat. Cats indeed have a sixth sense. Always jealous of me in the past, Mishi was uncharacteristically tender, sitting on my lap after my longer-than-usual absence. I summoned enough energy to go to the opera, but instead of spending money on dessert during intermission at the elegant Grand Tier Restaurant, I spent the money to hire a car to pick me up after the performances. In this way I could defy the cold and the snow. James Levine – he was not yet so ill – conducted Placido Domingo in *Othello.* I had set myself the goal of attending this performance while enduring my last chemotherapy regimens, so in addition to enjoying the opera, I felt a sense of accomplishment. I felt elated when crossing the expanse of Lincoln Center, facing the building's glass facade, peering in at the staircases, and seeing the crystal candle lights rise before the curtain. My daughter and granddaughter agreed to join me the next day for "*Tales of Hoffman,*" and their company yielded extra pleasure.

During my stay in New York, I celebrated another milestone: the fortieth anniversary of my arrival in the United States as an immigrant with my two children. Odile joined my celebration at a dinner at an Argentine restaurant. Having eaten large tenderloin steaks that night, we were better able to suffer the strict vegetarian restaurants we had to attend upon Anna's arrival. One of them served only "living food," which meant a menu of only raw, not cooked, vegetables. The discovery of a new French pastry shop in the neighborhood was more to my taste. It sold fresh "clafouties," fresh fruits, immersed in a sweet custard dough. Despite my fatigue, I also visited also the Metropolitan Museum.

Back home in Boston, I had other issues to ponder. I would soon be 75. My energy was not what it had been. Would I be able to, or would I even want to, go back to my demanding profession of more than 50 years? Could I – should I –work part time as a pediatrician? During the cold days in February as I pondered my fate, and my anxiety produced vivid dreams. In one, I had applied to medical school and it looked like I might be rejected. In another, I was still working at the Harvard School of Public Health, and I began to realize that research was not my calling. In still another dream, I was working at my old job at Dedham Medical Associates. The truth was that as I'd been accepted to medical school at 16, I'd now been in the field for more than 55 years. I'd never stopped working or studying. My father was a doctor, and medicine was my life. The practice of medicine had allowed me to earn a living while performing a service that created strong emotional ties between me and my patients. Could I even envision doing anything else?

A colleague who covered evenings at my office encouraged me to return, echoing my patients' hopes. Encouraged, I consulted with an experienced lawyer who informed me of the high risk of continuing to practice pediatrics at my age. Recent statistics published by the Harvard School of Public Health, based on studies of other branches of medicine, showed that the incidence of poor physician performance increased in proportion to the time elapsed since his or her graduation. I could not refute those statistics but I knew that since my graduation, I'd continually updated my knowledge. My association with Boston Children's Hospital kept me up to date, and it was my deepest wish to return to the practice of medicine.

On February 23, I celebrated my 75th birthday at a small party at the University Club, a gift from Odile. An ex-patient sent me a hat from Tours, France to cover my baldness. (My hair had yet to grow back.) Odile, two of my grandchildren, Zucu and Adal, and several friends celebrated with me. My son Marcelo arrived later for a visit which, unfortunately, was cut short by a big snow storm.

Buoyed by my culture-laden trips to New York, I applied for a volunteer position at the Boston Museum of Fine Arts (MFA) that I loved. Told that I would need to wait several months for the next training session, I felt a sense of inner urgency that gave me the courage to call the Director of Education. I outlined my experience visiting the MFA and other great world museums and she asked me to send her my resume. I did and began to receive emails listing opportunities at the museum for volunteers. Searching through them with Odile, I found one entitled, "Feeling for Form," a program to help the visually impaired enjoy the museum's treasures. Two elements of the work appealed to me. First, I relished the opportunity to further my knowledge of the museum's great works. Secondly, my father had been blind in his old age. Living far away, I was not able to be of much help to him. In this new position, at least I could help others in his situation. I met with Hannah Goodwin, the woman in charge of the program, and to my great joy I was accepted.

I began training to be a guide for the blind immediately. I also prepared written information about the museum's collections that I and other guides would use. The head of the museum's Accessibility Department suggested that my first tour focus on Egypt. I'd had the opportunity to visit the large Egyptian collection at the Met in New York. I explored the collections at both museums via the Brookline public library and the internet. The research gave me much peace and pleasure.

In April of 2005, despite my immersion in art and other activities, I decided to return to my pediatric practice. When I sat at my desk or examining a patient, I knew that at last my recovery was complete. The response of my patients was deeply gratifying. Even a baby I'd never treated gestured to be cuddled by me. Children express their parents' feelings; the baby was the second generation of patients in a family that I had cared for. Several patients had waited for my return to make important long-term decisions. In some cases, I had to disappoint them. I realized that I no longer had the energy to put in the long hours required. If I had to retire, I could leave this time without the drama involved during my absence due to cancer. It had been 51 years since my graduation from medical school and, above all, I was able to experience for one more time, the deep thrill of being back at work.

Anxiety about my health continued to plague me. We, cancer survivors, have a low threshold of anxiety when it comes to confronting health issues. I recall sitting at my desk studying, when I sensed something different about my toe. I looked and saw a small red spot. I looked two hours later, and it had a big red halo. I rushed to the emergency room where I was given an I.V. with antibiotics. They discovered an infection, the result of my impaired immunity – a problem others in my cancer survivor group had to deal with too. The episode weakened my strength, and I had to stay home from work for a day. The time flew as I prepared descriptions of Egyptian and Greco-Roman art for the visually-impaired visitors to the MFA. The work distracted me from my health problems and transported me into other, fantastic worlds.

On Mother's Day that year, all three of my children called. What a gift knowing that they were all well. In May of 2005, Odile and I attended the graduation of my grand-daughter Zucu, Marcelo's daughter, from Smith College. Zucu had studied for two years at a junior college before going on to Smith. Her "cum laude" graduation from Smith deserved a joyous celebration.

Meanwhile, the rhythm of care in my office changed. Appointments were scheduled for only a half hour and my schedule quickly filled. As usual, stories of my patients filled my head. Nonno, two-years old, and the youngest of four children whose parents had come from Nigeria, was an example. I met his mother at the birth of her first child while doing rounds for my colleagues at a suburban hospital. She had no assigned pediatrician. The nurses were not so patient with her, as it was difficult to understand her English and mannerisms. We seemed to click from that first visit, and as a result, she came regularly all the way from Mattapan. She always had a sweet smile, arriving with all her children on tow. She handled them in a relaxed and loving way. Occasionally she brought her mother who spoke no English. One day Nonno arrived for an appointment for a routine checkup. I noticed that the boy was not breathing well. Did he have a fever? I needed a diagnosis. His siblings waited patiently for my examination and for the results of x-rays and blood tests, concerned for the little brother. I discussed the possibility of an early pneumonia with his mother, explaining what signs to watch for, how contagious it could be for the rest of the family, and how to take the antibiotic I prescribed. I knew the father and the grandmother would help care for the children. A sense of caring and love imbued the visit. The siblings showed concern for their little brother with their quiet behavior, and their caring mother showed concern not only for her sick child but also for me, inquiring about my health.

Just as the visit was ending, my secretary rushed to tell me about a call that needed a prompt return. It was not a typical emergency call. In this case the mother was feeling desperate. Earlier that year, her only son Tony, sixteen, had gone to the railroad tracks with a friend to experiment with a "cool" idea. They decided playing on heavily electrified rail tracks would be fun. The results of this adventure were extensive burns that required several months of treatment at the Shiners' Burns Institute. His life was saved but he was left with extensive scars. The experience left emotional scars as well. The mother called to say that Tony was very depressed and refused to see his psychiatrist. The mother insisted that due to the boy's attachment to me, he would go if I recommended that he did. He had been under my care before the accident and during those difficult months after he had returned. Confronted with the consequences of his behavior, clearly he needed psychiatric care. I would have liked to have sat with him as I had many times, and allowed him time to tell me how he was feeling before referring him to a psychiatrist, but given my limited energy, I merely spoke to him over the phone, hoping that I was helpful.

On occasion, I thought of Florian, who died just before I was diagnosed with cancer. Whereas I felt liberated by his death from the nightmare of his last years, Odile continued to mourn his loss. A father whose mind was altered by disease had treated her cruelly and with parental detachment during his final years, but he still held a grip on her. Since it affected her, it continued to affect me.

Upon retiring from my medical practice, life began to open new vistas. I'd visited India in 2002 and it whetted my appetite to further explore Asia. I had saved for a trip I intended to take in February that would take me as far as Hong-Kong, but instead, the money had gone to pay for nurse assistants during my illness. The cruise company to whom I had paid a deposit gave me a credit and suggested several alternate itineraries. I decided to see more of Scandinavia and the Norwegian fjords. Having made arrangements at work, I embarked on my trip in June of 2005, my first travel since the illness.

Arriving in London, I felt an intense sense of awe that lasted throughout my stay there and I continued to feel deeply grateful to be alive during every day of that trip. Theo, an old friend from Argentina, joined me in London. Just as I had begun my residency in Argentina, Theo had ended his. He'd become one of the most respected clinicians in Buenos Aires. He also took care of my father devotedly and never charged a penny. His son, Alberto, continued caring for my father when I could not afford more private hospital stays for him. Alberto was the chief resident at an excellent community hospital. and he continued to care for my father, consulting with Theo, until my father's death. I owe my father's endurance to the age of 95 to their good care. I also by then had a personal relationship with Theo who'd been divorced for a couple of years at the time that Florian and I divorced. Theo invited me out which was possible because although he lived in Buenos Aires, his brother lived in Boston, so our paths crossed. At one point before he died, my father had hoped Theo and I might marry. But I decided to terminate the romantic relationship when Theo had said he would definitely not remarry. Years later, after my father's death, we started seeing each other again and traveled together.

We boarded the *Minerva* in Dover. Our cabin's full balcony provided better views than cabins with only a small porthole. I arose early to watch our arrival in Bergen, sitting at the big, round hall in the prow, protected by windows from the chill outside. A pale sun struggled to appear between the clouds. Initially, I could barely make out a few of the bigger islands and a few gray islets. As the boat began to approach them, the grey was transformed into green vegetation, and suddenly the small, wooden houses peppering the hills appeared. The city of Bergen presented a similar landscape from the ship, but the hills were taller and the larger islands were joined by bridges. Unfortunately, a typically rainy day disrupted our planned land tour. I would have liked to have met my dear friend Eva, who was born in Bergen and still had family there. Instead, Eva managed to have fine chocolates delivered to our boat.

The next day we cruised the Geiranger fjord in a tourist motor boat that navigated between two steep mountains, evergreen with rich vegetation, waterfalls, and small, wooden houses high on the slope. It was hard to imagine how people managed to climb those heights carrying whatever belongings they needed in that climate. During the ride back from the land we again experienced the dramatic beauty of the fjords and the sharply ascending hills. This sight was the highlight of my trip. Navigating further north, we arrived at Tromso, a university city that spends two months a year in darkness. We saw the modern, white "Artic Cathedral" and the tundra botanical garden with rocks and hardy, short bushes of different colors. The view reminded me of spring in Northern Canada as described by Barry Lopez, the American novelist and nature writer.

Next we anchored by the island of Spitsbergen, 770 miles from the North Pole. The temperature in the small town of Ny-Alesund was four-degrees Centigrade. Through the ship's enormous windows I could see the glaciers far away, all in diverse tones of gray. The landscape turned even more imposing as we headed back south, with its rows of steep black mountains interspersed with white glaciers. One glacier appeared to receive and reflect some unexpected sun and created a perfect setting for Wagner's "*Flying Dutchman.*" The surrounding mountains appeared to have faded in the clouds. Everything was gray again, including the ocean, immobile, without waves, as if it had solidified. A large piece of ice, broken away from a glacier, floated near us, a reminder that we had navigated extra miles to circumvent the neighboring large icebergs. Suddenly the sun came out again and the ocean turned blue, making the snow on the mountains appear whiter.

Our next call was at the island of Lakness with its idyllic, undulated landscape of sheep grazing on the hills that overlooked the bay. An eagle with wings extended flew above us. Nearby, under a millenary mound of earth, was a Viking museum that had been built in the shape of an upside down ship, housing the remains of adventurous Viking navigators. Enormous rocks surrounded the mound. A layer of earth and green pasture atop the museum insulated the primitive rooms below from the extreme temperatures, a system often used in this part of the world. While I visited this harsh land, I read *Independent People* by Harold Laxness, which describes the primitive Icelanders and their neighbors. The book helped me imagine life on the island. On the return voyage, we stopped at Alesund, a town that had burnt at the beginning of the 20th century and then was rapidly rebuilt in an elegant Art Deco style. Cranes in their nests on a roof added to the charm of our walk.

The cruise ended where it had started, in Dover. I had embarked only a few months after finishing my chemotherapy, and I felt well and in good company throughout the cruise. I appreciated that life still offered me such a happy time.

A second vacation I'd planned with my friend Theo, before my return to work. forced me to open a dialogue with my colleagues at DMA. The prospect raised the sticky issue of my future there. The few months I had spent back at work confirmed my fears that working part-time did not allow me to perform the totally dedicated pediatric work I had done in the past. There were other problems too. Some of my colleagues seemed more interested in taking charge of my practice than in supporting it. Many of my patients had waited for my return, preferring to discuss deep, pending issues with me on my return. That added to my concern because I knew I could no longer put in the hours I'd been used to.

Finally, to make things worse, in a meeting with only the medical director and the head of the group working in the Dedham office, I was told that the office could not schedule future appointments for me to be on call - "given my diagnosis of cancer." The comment put them in legal jeopardy as the law protected my right to work despite my diagnosis. Shocked and 75, I decided I no longer wanted to work in that environment. For years, I had struggled in various competitive atmospheres. Perhaps now was the time to leave. I let the managers know that I would retire from the practice of medicine the last day of October 2005. It was a hard decision, and what lay ahead was even harder. I needed to help my faithful patients make the transition to other doctors.

Before retiring, I had many gratifying experiences with my patients. Justin was an ex-patient of mine who had called and asked me to see his very ill newborn son. This baby became my patient, and I helped during his first years of life. Now they returned to see me with a healthy four-year- old and a new baby girl. What a joy was to see this family blooming.

As I accepted my decision and began the waning days of my practice, my work at the MFA blossomed. I was tested and then congratulated by my supervisor who observed my interaction with a visually impaired visitor who was allowed to touch a sculpture that could not be touched by the general public. In addition to this small victory, another one: I had my first haircut since my chemotherapy treatments! My new hairstyle was short and boyish, but everybody seemed to like it. I had waited so long for my hair to return, and here I was, having it cut – how ironic. I watched the small, white, curly pieces fall with unavoidable feelings of separation. I had hoped for them to reappear for so long.

I spent the beginning of August continuing the inevitable process of saying good-bye to my patients. Each patient's visit became a farewell ceremony. The children could not say very much but sensed some kind of change. Their unsmiling faces expressed understanding. Their mothers came with flower bouquets and tears. Many of the young adults, ready to expand their wings, could no longer count on seeing their long-time doctor. One who was already 18 and who had a boyfriend was sorry to hear the news — I had always been there for her, and she hadn't expected that situation would change. Meantime, I wondered if I would be able to spend three more emotionally charged months saying goodbye? Would I find another, equally worthy purpose?

Perhaps the hardest goodbye was to my patient who had been born with spina bifida, a severe disability in which the spinal cord is interrupted before birth and the lower part of the body is paralyzed. He was eighteen and had struggled since birth to live fully. I knew his future would not be easy. After I finished my exam, his devoted mother came to my private office to cry. I had to hold back my own tears, knowing that I would no longer be there to support them. How could I break a bond that had been such an important part of our lives to say, "I hope you will find a doctor to take good care of you?"

Changes were happening on other fronts. My "offer to purchase" a two-bedroom apartment in the same building in Brookline where I lived in a one-bedroom had been accepted. I needed more room. After my diagnosis, I'd needed constant home care, and there had been no space for nurse assistants, Odile, or friends who came to visit. Especially then when feeling weak and depressed, I had desperately needed space for myself. Now healthy again, I accepted financial help from my daughter, thinking that if remained healthy, I would have space for the many family and friends who might visit from all over the world. And if I became sick again, there would be space for caretakers.

During this period the news came from Argentina that my only brother Augusto had been diagnosed with cancer after an urgent operation for bowel intussusception. The ghost of cancer again hovered. My heart broke knowing he would need chemotherapy. Fourteen years prior, he had overcome melanoma and now faced another malignancy. The image of my mother, consumed and dying of cancer, reaffirmed the dangerous proclivity our genes carried. Would the two of us succumb to this disease too?

On the first anniversary of my diagnosis I learned that the cancer antigen CA 125 continued to be normal. I had been living in trimesters of hope separated by cancer antigen tests. "Perhaps I have one more year to live, something to cheer about," I thought. The first guided tour I performed at the museum made me believe that life would indeed be worth living. Studying art and servicing people provided me with emotional balance and opened new roads in my life.

In September, the weather was unsurpassed. Boston was in its glory. Every day I found time to go for a walk outdoors until my routine was suddenly interrupted by difficulty moving my bowels one morning. Trying to correct this problem, I created a worse one. I felt faint and could not stand. At the Brigham and Women's Hospital, I received intravenous fluids and, given my history, had a cat scan of my abdomen. Fortunately I was not diagnosed with a recurrence of my cancer but instead with a hernia at the site of my surgical wound. A hernia that could be repaired was not to be lamented. With the prospect of another surgery and the recent news of my brother's cancer, I had enough on my mind. These were my last weeks of saying farewell at my office, but I was preoccupied with illness, and I could not enjoy them.

That autumn I also attended an emotionally charged conference, "*Celebrating Survivorship*" at the Dana-Farber Cancer Institute where I had been treated. I was still on diapers from the last episode but I wanted to be there. Several survivors spoke, but I felt deeply for one named Patti. She was the head nurse at The Children's Hospital where I often saw patients. I listened and deeply admired her courage to keep up with her challenging job while fighting a killer like ovarian cancer. One bit of advice she offered was to go frequently to one's favorite places. Following her advice on a sunny afternoon, I went back to the "peaceful lake" near my home in Brookline. I had always viewed that wide open space as a real treasure. Scum, floating vegetation, covered the surface and trapped a million drops of water that produced a mirror-like reflection of the sun. By contrast, the green of the surrounding trees seemed deeper. It was a magical effect. While I walked around, the shining mantle disappeared, leaving only a light yellowish-green tone on the surface. In some patches, where the water was clear, a muddy bottom could be seen. A group of geese with elegant, long, black necks glided by. Three ducks swimming together drew parallel curves on areas of the water covered by tiny leaves. Around me, reddish dragonflies came and went. I thought about the conference I had attended, which had attracted three hundred participants. We heard about courageous women who were fighting for their lives and of their dedicated doctors. People always talk so much about God. This must be God: the dedication of those doctors to others and the faith, the hope and the strength to face life expressed by the women in that room. The survivors spoke also about the essential support received from friends and family. Everyone had gathered all their reserves to survive.

I packed up my office. It was October 23rd of 2005, the end of 34 years of dedicated work at DMA and 51 years in pediatrics. It was not easy to throw away my books – physician's guides that had been my faithful companions, available any time for consultation. They guided when I had been faced with decisions that would have a significant impact on the lives of my young patients. They were also silent witnesses to my concerns with difficult diagnoses. From their place on my office bookshelves they oversaw the diverse human encounters that had so often taken place. The papers I had to dispose of varied widely from amusing drawings to tragic reports like the one about my patient who was killed by a drunk driver. Down also came my diploma, henceforth meaningless, and the pictures I'd hung to soothe the children's fear of shots. In a drawer I found the photograph in a bucolic setting of the wedding of a nurse who had formerly worked for us. After she stopped working in our practice, she would drive a long distance to bring her children, already in their teens, to see me. I wondered what would replace those human connections.

On the 25th I stopped working. On the 26th I moved to my new, two-bedroom apartment, where my future as a retired physician would unfold. Fortunately, Odile's presence by my side allowed me, a bit over-whelmed, to face this final effort. And my blood tests provided further comfort by continuing to reassure me that my cancer had not recurred.

In New York, Odile and I went to see a rare revival of a famous ballet, "*The Green Table*," created by the German choreographer Kurt Joos in 1932. The ballet was created when the Nazis were becoming a political force and the League of Nations held its timid meetings as the specter of another war in Europe arose. My mother had taken me to see this powerful indictment of diplomats and of war, in Buenos Aires when I was seven years old. And now here I was with Odile as if completing a circle. Soon after seeing it, I began to study dance with an ex-member of the Joos ballet who had to escape his native Austria and who had found refuge in Argentina. Since the ballet still had contemporary significance, I could not avoid bitter reflection about the repeated and unavoidable wars that occurred during my lifetime and thoughts about the futile efforts of many, including artists, who warned of their consequences.

After five days of relaxation, I returned to the new apartment and the unpacked boxes and confronted my new life with a domesticity I had never known. The pile of boxes looked like an enticing first step. I decided to alternate unpacking with days off to read when I ignored all that needed to be done. It gave me a better feeling, and I began to settle down.

As the colorful foliage disappeared, I could see more bare branches. They have a beauty of their own but they announce more severe weather and a more reclusive life.

If I'd had any doubts about my performance as a pediatrician and how it had affected my patients, a farewell party at DMA in November left me reassured that I did not waste my productive years or choose the wrong profession.

A note had been sent to my patients and also published in the local paper saying that on November 14, I would receive those who had not had a chance to say good-bye to me. A packed line of parents, grandparents and children waited for more than forty-five minutes to greet me. There were hugs, kisses and tears for more than two and a half hours. When I thought about it afterwards, I could not believe it had happened. Even personnel from my office, some who had left long ago, were there. I remembered every detail about each one of them, and this made seeing them especially vivid. There was the tall medical student who had been my patient since birth; the lovely young adolescent who had many health problems of her own and whose ambition was to follow in my footsteps and become a pediatrician; the two very young sisters, angelical in their beauty, daughters of my ex-patient, who painted two canvasses because they knew that I now worked at the MFA and I was interested in art. I returned home with eight bouquets of flowers and plants and boxes of gifts. The next morning I was up at 4:30, still in a state of deep emotion, opening cards and gifts, inundated by expressions of love.

With daughter Odile at a retirement party given by colleagues

My work at the MFA continued and kept me involved. My commitment as a volunteer did not diminish. I gave the museum all that my physical condition and mental abilities allowed. When unable to work as a guide due to physical limitations, I wrote and prepared materials for other guides.

My passion for reading and learning never ebbed, and my visual memory helped me renew pleasures in the field, most recently, of plastic arts. The opportunity to attend operas in New York continues to be a source of special pleasure for me. Opera, the only art whose exact beginning we can trace – to 1568 – combines drama, music, costumes, history and scenery. Opera lifts our emotions and delights our ears and eyes.

More adventures awaited me in November when I met the student who was going to become my mentee during the 2005-2006 academic year. Our meeting was part of an interesting program at Harvard College conducted by the Radcliffe Alumni Association. The program addressed the issue of combining careers with family roles from the perspective of medical students. I had already mentored two young women, one of whom was in her second year of medical school. This year, no girl selected me! Instead, a young male student, one of the few in the program, selected me as his mentor. He explained his choice, saying that he wanted to have a grandparent figure in this country since his parents were from India. If this is what he wanted, he made a wise choice. I was old enough to be his grandmother, and I was an immigrant myself. His situation paralleled that of my own American daughter Odile, who also had foreign parents and no extended family. Yet I wasn't sure I could make a contribution advising him about medical school, since both of his parents were doctors, and his mother was also a pediatrician. This charming, young man was intelligent and educated. He was about to begin working on a project at the emergency room of The Children's Hospital that involved patient interviews. I had a surge of envy when I heard what he was about to do, yet thrilled for him, because I knew the Boston Children's Hospital Emergency Room is an exciting place for a doctor.

Merciless December! Two big storms confirmed that winter was near and surrounded me with snow and ice – elements that I never could deal with easily despite the many years I lived in Boston. The sidewalks were as treacherous as the driving, and I feared that my current short period of time without health problems would be interrupted by an accident. I wanted to fly away from this picturesque white landscape and find ground that would be firmer beneath my feet.

Financial issues now arose as a major concern. I had dreams about my dear father who had always been there as my financial benefactor. I dreamed almost daily, and often I remembered parts of my dreams. My father had been my financial support for so many years that I turned to him once more in a dream. I asked for a couple of dollars to go back to his home. My dreams were vivid and clearly expressed my newest anxiety: the worry that my disability funds would only last one year because of my age – an important detail never disclosed during all the years I paid for disability coverage. I'd counted on these funds to retire only to discover now they were non-existent.

In my dream, the houses were of medium height with no intervals of green, and they had a traditional European look, as one would see in Buenos Aires or in an Italian city like Milan. The buildings were narrow with two or three stories and iron balconies. Time had done a job on those concrete facades, and they all had the same grey or washed out creamy color. It was dark in my dream and I knew it was not safe to walk alone, so I asked my father for money for transportation. It is interesting that I was asking him for help again, asking for money when fears for my financial future arose.

10

Beginning Retirement

Early in 2006, and newly retired that winter, I decided to take a restorative trip to Italy, a country that has always been a favorite of mine. I had a dear nephew, Martin, there, and I had always dreamed of visiting him for a longer period than the two or three days allowed when I worked full time. I spent three special weeks with Martin and his lovely wife, Grazia. They were good, intelligent and loving people, and I enjoyed helping them take care of their new baby, Daniele, and I also had a chance to see the other child and how Davide had grown. After all, it had been more than 35 years since I had enjoyed the care of my own small infants. During my visit, Georgina came from Switzerland for a weekend. We walked and chatted in Varese; we stopped at one of the "pasticcerias" with pastries in the windows that make you sigh with lust. We visited book shops and saw titles of renowned Italian authors. I bought a book in Italian, eager to reinvigorate my language skills as well.

A highlight of the trip was a visit to an exhibition at the Palazzo Reale of Milan dedicated to Caravaggio and his influence in Europe. Not far from it was "*il Duomo*" with its stunning, lacy, white structure which contrasted with the day's blue sky. At the old and venerable opera theater of Cuomo, I heard several of the most talented young opera singers on the continent.

Back in Boston, I grew busy – so busy sometimes that I could not slow down. I also grew grateful – for health and for having the energy to work at my new job as a volunteer at the Museum of Fine Arts. When weather permitted, I took long walks and got back in touch with nature, which I also viewed as a gift. Family visits too were a gift.

Cultural events continued to enrich my life. In sunny May, I went to the opera to see *Thays* by Massenet. Attending opera has always been a religious experience for me: the music, the staged drama and the voices take me to other worlds. *Thays*, a story of sensual love as opposed to sacred love, made me think about my own conflicts with sex. Perhaps women in their mature years are not supposed to write about sex, but how can we not analyze and discuss this vital aspect of our existence? And so, I write briefly about my thoughts after the hours in which I sat entranced, listening to that opera. For a long time I had renounced sex. I knew that I could not have sex if I was not in love, and yet finding love was never easy for me. During the years when my second marriage was failing, I had no option but to give up sex except for a few distressing encounters. But my erotic dreams recurred, and with them came romantic feelings evoked by past sexual relationships. My dreams reminded me of the poor monk's conflicts that are dramatized in *Thays*.

I see the Christian emphasis on denying the joy of sex as a curse. But the promiscuity some people practice may also be a curse. Sex is such an intimate and important piece of our lives, yet we have few rules that we can trust to guide our decisions.

Attending the opera, reading, and visiting museums is important to me, but family is paramount. On his way from Europe back to California, Marcelo's son, Adal, then in his twenties, paid me a visit. It was a thrill. as were all visits from my four grandchildren. The boy was tall and handsome and a delightful guest. His father was a charmer, and so, it appeared, was the son. Adal had a difficult childhood but had apparently emerged from that drama with wisdom and an appreciation of the important things. The weather matched our moods: it was late spring in Boston and delightful.

Odile, too, was better able to get on with her life now that she knew I was well. That June, Georgina arrived for a scientific meeting in Boston. Georgina was very interested in my health and followed my diet closely. When I told her not to worry about a gene test I took, in her usual direct way Georgina answered, "I worry about my genetic charge – not about yours." She was helping to open new frontiers in treatments and doing research at the highest levels. I was gratified seeing her doing it, and it did not matter to me anymore that I hadn't been able to succeed doing research. Her visit was especially welcome as it occurred on June 14, the fifth anniversary of my dear father's death.

A day before Georgina arrived, I had heard from her daughter, Anna, then 27. She, too, had news. She said she was planning to leave Guatemala, where she had been living and was rethinking commitment to the sect that had devoured her for the last seven years. During our visit, Georgina and I shared the hope that Anna was coming to terms with her life and that we might all feel less desperate about her choice.

I'd also heard from Marcelo who called more often. During one call he informed me that he had changed companions. His new relationship turned out to be long lasting and one that suited him well.

Over the years, I followed the vicissitudes in the lives of my children and grandchildren with devoted interest. Despite the distances, I shared their joys and worries. I appreciated living in the modern era – so different from the one of my ancestors when distances and physical separation meant irreparable losses.

The work at the MFA helped occupy my time, but one day it occurred to me that my workload had decreased. Like many people, I believed that, as Irving Stone said in *The Agony and The Ecstasy*, "A man is as old as his creative forces within him." I needed to produce to have peace of mind. On a day when I felt particularly depressed about my lack of work, I received a moving email from Hannah, the head of the department at the MFA. It said that she enjoyed working with me because I was smart and open, and she thanked me for being patient with her. I was so relieved, and yet I wondered why had I been so worried about my lack of involvement in a productive activity?

Writing a diary helped calm me, but I often wondered how much of what I wrote would be of interest to others? Despite that concern, I continued to write. I felt that I simply could not live without the discipline of writing – especially in my later years. It didn't matter if my writing failed to satisfy critical expectations.

My dedication to the MFA was fulfilling. We usually prepared our guided tours based on information we received from our coordinator. One day, instead of the five mildly disabled but sighted young adults I'd expected, my only visitor was a twelve-year-old with cerebral palsy. He was unable to talk or to easily fix his eyes on any object or on me when I spoke to him. He communicated with his mother with a shake of his hand. The coordinator of this group, who had organized the boy's visit, was a blind young man. At the last minute, he decided to join us and proved to be an eager learner. I improvised a successful tour of the Egyptians' great sculptures for the two of them. I had to forget my own concerns and concentrate to being flexible and creative in meeting their special needs.

During the summer of that year, Odile and I flew to the Galapagos Islands. Being with my daughter was life's gift to me since the day she was born. On vacation together and joined by a cousin from her father's side, we united in an earthly paradise. After lunch one day, I met a physician who remembered having called me from Argentina many years ago when she needed information about emigrating to the United States. I was glad to learn from her that she recalled our conversation as useful. She had not forgotten my name.

Back home, I regularly attended meetings of the group of survivors of gynecologic cancers. The members were both my support and my teachers since they helped me deal with new physical and emotional experiences. I developed strong attachments to some of them whose agony filled pages of my diary. As a doctor, I had an ability I didn't enjoy. I foresaw their ominous future when they commented on a symptom or on recent test results. Worrying about their risk of death muffled my own fear. Giving them support or being upset about their risks was easier than to focus on my own anxiety.

One of them, Michele, as I had mentioned earlier, was clearly approaching death and as she did, my pain for her increased. I'm sure my emotions had deep roots in seeing my mother dying when I was a child. The death of Carolyn, whom I had met briefly at a yearly "*Celebration of Life*," had a big impact on me and left me feeling that I had not given her enough support. Like my mother, she died of pancreatic cancer. Like a child, I took to drawing to release my anguish. Coming back from one of those painful meetings, I went on line and found Matisse's *La Danse*. Holding hands, the twisted silhouettes dance in a circle. It reminded me of our group. In the same manner, we were trying to stop death from entering our circle. With that in mind, I made a drawing which I brought to the group's next meeting. Despite my poor technique, the image appeared to impact everyone in our group and their reactions inspired me to take classes in drawing.

That fall, I read *The Story of Edvard Munch*, by Ketil Bjornstad. A biography, it concentrated on revealing Munch's feelings during important episodes in his life. Reading it encouraged me to describe the deep feelings the MFA tours I led aroused in me. For one tour, my colleague and I, both inexperienced with this kind of visitor, had expected a group of three deaf-blind visitors and five interpreters, plus the person in charge. The group leader was also partially hearing and visually impaired. We were both shocked when the group arrived with seven more than expected. Several were deaf and communicated through sign language. The group consisted of the young and the old, the blind and the deaf, and the deaf only. There was an almost equal number of whites, African-Americans and one Latino (two including myself). All were animated – an exciting crowd – but it was difficult for me to imagine how I would organize their visit. Despite the challenge, or perhaps because of it, I was inspired. They inspired me. They were a large group with serious physical limitations but were so enthusiastic it would bring tears to anybody's eyes. One by one, I stopped at the sculptures visitors were allowed to touch with gloves and I described what I thought was most important about them – aided by their well-trained translators. The translators communicated using a modified American sign language on the palms of the hands. Everybody was fascinated with one sculpture in particular: Sekhmet, the Egyptian goddess of healing.

A month later, in October of 2006, I led a tour of seven people afflicted with Alzheimer's. As a physician, I must note that 2006 was the one hundredth anniversary of the first description of this disease by the eponymous and distinguished German neurologist, Dr. Alois Alzheimer. Two days before the tour, I'd attended a meeting in New York that commemorated the date. It is sad to reflect that we still cannot prevent or cure Alzheimer's. Dr. Alzheimer described with precision the pathologic findings in the brain tissue of his patients after their death. Yet a century later, the current recommendations to avoid succumbing to this kind of brain destruction are even vaguer than those suggested to keep a healthy heart.

My visitors were attentive and polite and seemed to be following my talk for about forty minutes. We stayed in the American Decorative Arts room where I showed them sculptures and paintings. I told them stories about the artists and described their works. They seemed to focus better on the anecdotes of the lives of the painters and sculptors than on their work. At some point during the tour, I saw that several of the visitors were looking at the furniture on display. I had been careful to read the descriptions of the pieces earlier so I could explain the prevailing French style. One of the visitors commented that her grandmother had a dining room piece like the one in the exhibit. She said it made her feel at home in that room. I will never know how much they understood and most likely, they will not remember any of it. But they definitely had fun, which made the tour worthwhile. Before leaving, one of the visitors who had made many appropriate comments, asked what town we were in. Her question reminded me of the formidable gaps in memory they experienced.

I had had only one prior experience regarding Alzheimer's at the museum. One Sunday the previous year, in early November 2005, I'd read a long article in the *New York Times* about the effects of art on patients with Alzheimer's. The article had a photograph of a group of patients in front of a famous Picasso painting at the Museum of Modern Art in Manhattan. It also mentioned that a similar program existed at Boston's MFA and that my MFA supervisor, Hannah Goodwin, was an expert on how art can affect Alzheimer's patients. I congratulated her by phone, and she told me that she would like to talk to me about her work. She later told me that many people had read the article, and she had received a call from a member of the museum whose wife was afflicted with Alzheimer's. He wanted to try to visit the museum with her. Hannah asked me if I would lead the tour, and I was provided an individual lecture for over an hour on how to conduct it.

My medical training as a pediatrician did not include much on Alzheimer's illness, and the limited personal experience I'd had to that point was an occasional meeting with my stepmother who had a mild case of it. I decided to learn more about Alzheimer's disease and called a friend who is famous for his research on the subject. My friend referred me to the psychotherapist who treats Alzheimer's patients. She was kind enough to have lunch with me and tell me about her experiences. She gave me material to read.

I learned that my future visitor had been an abstract painter, a school of art that had never appealed to me. I used to cross the gallery featuring the American Expressionists without stopping to look at them. Now to prepare, I went to the gallery, and after studying each of the paintings, made a selection of the ones I would show. I found a good book about the origins of abstract painting and material about the American painters who were on display. I learned to recognize every painting in the museum's Lane collection.

The morning of the tour I felt queasy. My limited experience with Alzheimer's patients prepared me for possible failure. Traffic was worse than ever, and I arrived with little time to relax or even to check my coat. Entering through the side door of the museum, I saw a blond woman sitting in a wheelchair pushed by a young Afro-American woman. They had exited a car driven by a man who was obviously about to park it. I thought that the fact that we were all arriving at the same time was a good omen. I met them as scheduled at the Information Center. I greeted the blond woman warmly and commented on the beautiful silver necklace she was wearing. She smiled. She was petite and had straight hair and bangs which framed her blue eyes. She had a small nose and fine lips. She appeared well-groomed and dressed with obvious care. Her husband walked by her side. He was dressed informally but conservatively. They were a handsome pair.

I explained that we would pass by several exhibits before going to the one we wanted to see, yet I stopped in front of an exhibit featuring Middle-America gold. It was so stunning that it had to impact her in some way, I thought. She looked at it but said nothing. We went on to the Lane collection, with American art from the early 20th century. I began showing a series of paintings by Charles Dove. His colors were soft. I described each one, using information I had read and adding my own thoughts about colors or forms. She paid attention to all the paintings. After seeing the third or fourth painting, my visitor began to make comments. Her husband, knowledgeable on the subject of abstract art, participated and addressed her tenderly, encouraging her comments. We completed a visit of fifty minutes with her sustained interest and listened to several of her remarks, all-appropriate. As I was progressing to more complicated images, she stopped talking. She rejected a Stuart Davis painting with loud colors and busy designs, as I had been warned might happen. It was too busy, probably confusing, perhaps even frightening for her.

At this point I asked her again if she was tired, if she would like to see some paintings of Sergeant, or if she would prefer a cup of tea. She wanted a cup of tea. She expressed herself in a delicate manner that I found charming. We went to the cafeteria, and I chatted with her a bit about the garden. Everything went smoothly. Her husband attended to her attentively, and he took time to tell me more about her. He had brought pictures of her paintings for me to keep and also spoke about their past as a couple. I had started the tour with a woman unable to talk, and we ended with a pleasant social encounter. The visit to the museum had brought her back to life. When our meeting was over, I was deeply moved and felt as if I had been present at a miracle, although I knew it would be short-lived.

A *Rhyme* from G. A. Becquer, the Spanish poet, has hunted me since their visit:

Rhyme VII

In a dark corner of the salon,
perhaps forgotten by its owner,
silent and covered with dust lay the harp.

How many notes slumber in its strings
like birds sleeping in a branch awaiting the snowy hand
that knows how to pluck them out.

Ai!- I thought-how many times
genius sleeps thus at the bottom of the soul,
and, like Lazarus, waits for a voice
to command it: " arise and walk."

More and more my work at the MFA consumed my life and opened new areas of knowledge. I learned of The Carroll Center for the Blind, for example, which, since 1936, has provided training to individuals of all ages who have lost their sight. Located in Newton, Massachusetts, The Center often sent trainees to the MFA. On July 2009, a group of six blind trainees visited. The tour included music and our responses to it. We started with an 18th Century painting of a poet playing a lyre, followed by the colorful "*Jazz*" of Stuart Davis, an important American painter and print maker. We stopped and described the four figures dancing a minuet in a 19th Century painting. Soon, we were all dancing. The excitement progressed as we moved on to a contemporary video of a man singing rock with a microphone in his hand. The experience was so rousing that one of the visitors, of very short stature, and who had arrived in a wheelchair, managed to arise and join the dance. I had to hold back tears. She later made a poster with the word "music" on top and wrote on it all the emotions that music inspires.

The Perkins School for the Blind, in Watertown, Massachusetts, also has many programs, among them a residential or day program for children and adolescents. Groups from the school visited the MFA on a regular basis. Their visits were cherished by the visitors and their guides as well. I remember in particular one visit that took place in July of 2008. My supervisor, Hannah Goodwin, organized the program. The tour took place at the African gallery and included stories about the objects and masks on exhibition behind glass. We viewed textiles and heard a drummer on different types of drums. The tour ended with a drum performance and the blind students participated.

Another amazing episode: viewing the unique blown glass works of Dale Chihuli. The American sculptor exhibited his works at the MFA in 2011. At the request of Hannah Goodwin, Chihuli created eight single pieces that could be touched by our visually impaired visitors. In one tour, I was asked to be the assistant who handles the pieces. But because of my sciatica, I did only two tours of Chihuli's installations.

One morning in June, four teenagers with cognitive deficiencies arrived in wheelchairs with their aides. We met at the large atrium when suddenly I was asked if I would guide one of the teenagers myself instead of simply handing objects to his museum guide. This was an unexpected change of plans. The young man was visually impaired and cognitively disabled and he was non-verbal. He appeared to be about 16 years old and sat in his wheel chair, bent down, with his head falling. Incapable of speech and drooling, he seemed unaware of his environment. His very experienced aid seemed to understand and then interpret for him despite the fact that he could not talk. I began by letting him touch the pieces of glass one by one. At times, I would need to direct his hands because he had difficulty with motility, and his hands were small for his age. Did he ever use them on his own, I wondered? I tried to be gentle but also enthusiastic as I encouraged him to feel for textures and shapes. At one point, he began to raise his head and swing it rapidly to the left. The aid explained that it meant he liked what we were doing. He continued repeating this gesture while touching all the pieces. Next I had to take him to the galleries where the exhibition was. Could he hear and understand my descriptions in the middle of that noisy crowd? I kneeled next to him and spoke softly into his ear, telling stories inspired by the different exhibits. He seemed to listen attentively. Ignoring whether he understood my words or liked the experience, I kept talking. When the tour ended, his aid asked him to let me know if he liked the tour. He lifted his head, turned it towards me, and with a big effort, he emitted a sound to thank me. I left him feeling very moved and rushed to find a private corner where I could take in my emotions. I don't know at what level, or in what world, but we had been able to communicate.

Thanksgiving and the Holidays – 2006

As the end of 2006 approached and the Thanksgiving season began, I recalled how I'd celebrated the holiday over many years. I remembered Thanksgivings and other holidays when, on call for my office, I had to juggle family and work responsibilities. Those recollections fill me with a mix of emotions. I remember holidays when we lost friends or family.

One Thanksgiving in 1969 when I was pregnant with Odile, I used a rolling pin to bake. It triggered my first bout of neck radiculitis, a problem that would reoccur for the rest of my life. That year we lost a friend a few days after our dinner. His homosexuality was unacceptable then and losing his job was the last straw. After another Thanksgiving years later, a dear cousin called to let me know about the self-inflicted death of her son. I remember my lonely drive to Northampton, Florian having refused to join me, my heart heavy and snow on the road. After my divorce, I spent one of the hardest Thanksgivings with a family whose son, a Marine, had been my patient. The son had died when his parachute failed to open. For many people, depression worsens during holidays.

I also recalled Thanksgiving in 2004. Odile and I spent the holiday alone. I lay in bed, feeling destroyed by my fourth chemo, physically and emotionally exhausted, when unexpectedly, a neighbor knocked at our door bringing plastic containers with food – a show of kindness we both badly needed. I had much to be grateful for.

11

Getting to Now

Retirement allows me to enjoy the best of two worlds: my adopted home in America and the land of my birth. Escaping Boston winters and commuting to Buenos Aires is now a regular occurrence. When in Boston, the MFA continues as the center of my activities, interrupted by periodic trips to Odile's home in Manhattan. My children and grandchildren visit occasionally in Boston where we hold what I call our "Thanksgiving reunions," though held at odd times and in warmer weather. My frequent travel companion, Theo, died of an acute illness in 2009. We had ended our romance but remained good friends until his death.

I cherish both my homes. My home in Boston houses my books, records, paintings, and whatever is left of my successive past lives. Its setting borders an old estate with ancient trees, flowers, birds, and nearby ponds, and is perfect for my daily walks. I see only green from my wide windows. My home in Buenos Aires, one Odile generously chose for me, is within walking distance of Palermo, with its miles of woods, endless parks and lakes. The building was designed by a famous architect. Glass doors lead out to a long balcony that permits frequent al fresco meals. From the top of the building, there is a stunning view of the river and the city. Here I have a second chance to be among my large family and a few friends I left behind fifty years ago.

Intermittent pain, however, became a new protagonist in my story. Since I returned from Europe the summer of 2007, and until I had an operation in May of 2013, I suffered from severe sciatic pains in both legs. My condition is common among the elderly and is called spinal stenosis. It dictated what I could do and when and how I did it.

Beginning in December of 2012, my pain intensified until it turned me into a non-ambulatory patient. At home, I would drag myself from room to room and with difficulty, to a car. It took all my determination to stand just to wait for a taxi. I purchased a cane so that I could grab onto something to help me withstand the pain. The pain grew so great that I began having suicidal fantasies and even found myself ruminating about what height I should jump from. I sought medical help, but I refused to load myself with drastic medications. Walking in the pool, a temporary measure, helped keep me moving.

Pain diminished my energy, and a lack of energy made it hard to plan activities. Every aspect of my daily life demanded extra concentration and a special effort to the point that I became inpatient with myself and needed to remind myself of the natural limitations age and illness impose. When not in pain, I feared the return of the pain. Only when I was eventually relieved of it after surgery did I come to realize how profound and pervasive its destructive effects had been.

Although I dreaded surgery, it seemed like a logical next step. I'd read the medical literature on spine surgery and knew the statistics and that the success rate for such procedures was poor. Comments from survivors were not inspiring either. In the end, however, I decided that I had no choice. Pain impaired my every step, and I did not want to be confined to an electric wheelchair for the rest of my life.

I was operated on in New York on May 14th of 2013. I relied on Odile to choose the surgeon, and she chose Dr. Robert Snow. He gave me a new lease on life. Returning to a world without pain helped me realize the deep and widespread effect of pain on the sufferer.

While in Buenos Aires, during the summer of 2011-2012, and seeking a group with whom to exchange ideas, I encountered instead an intellectual, a man full of exciting ideas. Enrique Dunayevich was two years my senior. I'd met him briefly when I was an adolescent, and then, now, in this later state of life, we met again. I helped Enrique arrange to have one of his books published in the United States. Preparing it for publishing was a long and arduous process and during it, we fell in love. I could not believe the intensity of our feelings. It was an exciting, romantic adventure, totally unexpected at our ages, with Enrique navigating his motor boat through an enchanting delta to the house designed and decorated with his own hands. We had not expected this adventure and knew not what life would bring us next. As long as there is life, life can surprise us.

While I was falling in love in Buenos Aires that summer, it was winter in New York, and while walking her dog in Central Park, Odile met Tim Gordon. A relationship that developed slowly and included Tim's two children, culminated in marriage on October 19, 2013. For many weeks after their initial meeting, Odile and Tim walked their dogs together before ever going out on an official date. Tim also waited for a long time before he introduced his two children to Odile. His wife had died of cancer a few years before, and he was both the mother and father to them. His life had elements that reminded me of my own after my mother died. Odile was sensitive, humble and loving to Tim and his two children.

Odile organized an unconventional, unpretentious and most wonderful wedding. Arrows of love crossed in all directions at the ceremony. Like the shining goddess Diana, Odile initiated the arrows while also managing to take care of her guests so all felt loved. The result was a memorably warm encounter that included many of my loved ones: my children, grandchildren, a second cousin, and the grandchild of a dear friend.

The ceremony took place at the imposing Church of St. Ignatius in Manhattan, led by a priest who seemed both kind and intelligent. I walked Odile down the aisle, honored to be the one to give her away. She was dressed simply but stunningly. Paul, Tim's oldest child, was his best man, and a brother of Tim and three of my grandchildren did readings. I felt proud of my grandchildren. My heart seemed to enlarge, and I felt as if I'd witnessed a small part of myself in all of their beauty. When the vows were said, I walked back down the aisle behind Tim and Odile, with Paul on one arm and Charlie, the youngest of Tim's children, on the other, moved by the privilege.

After church we went to an historic Italian Renaissance House for a party, where before entering, we were greeted by the dogs that had started this union. My family and our friends joined in the celebration with Tim, his friends and members of his late wife's family.

My own family prospered and grew. Adding to our good news, my granddaughter Anna Penayo, Georgina's daughter, gave birth to a beautiful little girl on May 26th of 2013. Her name is Anime Vega and during the last few days of 2013, I had the privilege of seeing Anime for the first time and watching the new mother bloom. And while finishing these pages, during a brief visit to Oslo, I saw Anime take her first steps.

My passion for reading and learning never ebbed, and my visual memory helped me renew pleasures in the field, most recently, of plastic arts. The opportunity to attend operas in New York continues to be a source of special pleasure for me. (Opera the only art whose exact beginning some trace to a specific date. It happened in 1568 at the spectacular wedding of Duke Wilhem V of Bavaria to Renata of Lorraine. During the banquet, the successive pieces of music were accompanied by allegoric, live scenes. They were followed by the *Florentine Intermedi,* before scenes and vocal music acquired an opera format.)

Finally, and last but not least, writing has filled the gaps in my time. How delightful it has been to be employed in all these manners.

Now in my eighties, I ask myself this: If I were to depict my life on a graph, what shape would it take? The lines probably would climb smoothly from zero until my early adolescence and then zigzag, indicating a cataclysm. That disruption would reflect my mother's illness and her death when I was twelve. Those adolescent years of my chart would be interlaced with the story of our survival, but as a heartbroken family. Though lacking maternal direction and learning to care for many of my own personal needs, I continued to benefit and learn from my father's values and interests. Money was not discussed; he provided the essentials for years to come. But my dear father taught me about giving and respecting other people, and about the rewards of caring for patients. He exposed me to literature, history and music. My ballet studies had already implanted classical music in my muscles and ears. What a rich fountain from which to drink, my father offered me. I also had the good fortune to inherit some of my father's spiritual energy; whether it was the result of chemicals concocted in the liver or the brain – I don't know.

The graph after my early girlhood and young adult years splits into two lines. One line objectively represents the historical events I narrate in this book. The other line, perhaps shown in a lighter hue and with a higher wave frequency, would signify my emotional ups and downs. The lighter tone of its curve would represent a kaleidoscope of ongoing joys and anguishes; the chest constriction many of us feel when aware of our attachment to our parents; our worries for the health and happiness of our children, and of course the highs that learning, art, working, and loving produce – all of the emotional states that light up our memories.

I lived during two centuries, both characterized by accelerated change. Since youth, my sympathies have favored the revolutionary winds that have passed through women's issues and politics. At fifteen I rebelled against the repression of early Perónism, the roots of the political beliefs that marked my future inclinations. A government that threatened human rights was unacceptable to me, and as a Jew, I could hardly ignore horrific world events during the Nazi-Fascist ascent. Craving peace and dreading violence in any form are values woven into my very being. My interest in national and international events never waned although my participation has been intermittent, and in my mature years, I did not have the full passion manifested by some of my dear friends whom I so admire. Yet my deep concern for the needs of the most vulnerable human beings remains as strong as ever.

Programs like PAVE, Pediatricians Against Violence Everywhere, organized by medical residents and students at the American Academy of Pediatrics, make me feel that my efforts to prevent violence are still having an important impact.

When I look back on my education, it is remarkable that I earned a doctoral degree in Argentina. The fees I paid as a medical student were modest, and while I had some good teachers at public school, I had some great ones in medicine. I was privileged in recent years to associate with people who taught me art, a field in which my own passion for reading and my strong visual memory has helped me. These diverse opportunities and the pleasure derived from them created a commitment to sow knowledge and experience whenever I could. It also linked me to young people at my advanced age, here and abroad – links I treasure.

In a special way, I must also point out that my mother's early death, reinforced by my own cancer at age 74, was also an important part of my education. It taught me to appreciate life even during its most difficult moments.

I am not religious, and I did not have any religious upbringing. I was exposed to the moral content of my Jewish tradition, though I went on living without religion. That said, I consider that every human being has the right to be respected for his beliefs, as long as those beliefs respect those of others and strive for harmony. We can tolerate and even rejoice that beliefs can be so diverse. I recall that the ancient Egyptians believed in a judgment that occurs after death. At the time of judgment, they believed, men appear before a scale. The goddess Ma'at, who signifies cosmic harmony and equilibrium, is on one platform of the scale. The heart of the deceased is on the other platform. When one's behaviors are weighted, the result grants eternal life – or not.

How similar the Egyptian principle is to the mandate of Moses' "Tables of Law," when it comes to codes of conduct, or the Christian belief in paradise or hell. So have others, including the 20th century mystic and philosopher Simone Weil, who referred to "Le Pesanteur et la Grace," – that our actions and ideas either elevate us or pull us lower. I have always believed that man is born with an innate sense of good and bad. It's up to us to choose and alter the directions of our lives. My work with children for more than fifty years has only strengthened that conviction.

I suppose all in all you might categorize me as a humanist, surmising that I espouse recognizing nature's beauty and gifts; living harmoniously within our community of human beings, valuing knowledge and our intellectual and cultural inheritance, and valuing the enormous significance of love. But most important to me, I value service. Rabindranath Tagore, the Nobel-prize-winning Indian poet, wrote:

> "I slept and dreamt that life was joy.
> I awoke and found that life was service.
> I acted and, beheld, service was joy."

When I look back on my life, I would also add a word about aging. I think a great deal about the difficulties of growing older. The older one gets, the harder it is to connect with those younger than us. The fast changes in social patterns and in the ways we communicate make older people feel isolated. In addition, when I connect with those close to my own age, I find them struggling endlessly with health problems. Growing older is not an easy path. The elderly I meet remind me that, as we cross the Styx River toward our final destination, we seldom have a smooth ride in Charon's boat. We swim laboriously, occasional elegant strokes alternate with difficult gasps to go on. Some moments we can feel the old pleasures, but at others, we nearly drown, depressed and in pain. This dreadful condition increases our sense of isolation. We need our inner energy to walk straight, but most of all, we need love to encourage our uphill march.

"Yet, as I have lent a hand to others, I find many to support me in my efforts to enjoy and give meaning to my life. I hope to continue to contribute in some way as I have done before. As Nikki Giovanni said well in *The Life I Led*, "I hope I die warmed by the life I tried to live."

What is going to be my next task?

April 23, 2015 Luisa Stigol

About the Author

Luisa Stigol's life and memoir reflect her passions: for study, her efforts to see a world without prejudice or violence, and her sincere caring for others. She has additionally embraced two avatars: that of a woman in medicine and that of a mother to three children.

She was born in Buenos Aires, Argentina in 1930, graduating as a Doctor in Medicine in 1954 from the School of Medicine, National University of Buenos Aires. Stigol was appointed to the National Council of Scientific and Technical Research (Consejo Nacional de Investigaciones Cientificas y Tecnicas). Years later, her doctoral thesis about breathing in chronic poliomyelitis patients, brought her to relocate her family to Boston where, in 1962, she became a Fellow at the Department of Physiology at the Harvard School of Public Health. Three years later, Stigol returned as Research Associate at the same Department. In 1968, she became Fellow in Pathology at Boston Children's Hospital, and in 1973, she returned to the practice of pediatrics at Dedham Medical Associates, where she worked for thirty-four years.

Stigol was awarded the von L. Meyer Award at the Department of Pathology of Children's Hospital.

Additionally, she was active in the prevention of violence, and among other such activities, appointed as Principal Investigator of the Violence

Prevention Project of the Harvard Community Health Foundation in 1991. In 1993, she became a member of the new Committee on Domestic Violence of the Massachusetts Medical Society (MMS).

In 1994, Stigol was given the "Women in Medicine Award" of the MMS.

Today, Stigol resides in Boston where she continues volunteer work as a docent for the Boston Museum of Fine Arts.

Made in the USA
Las Vegas, NV
06 October 2021